THE INHERITANCE

Joann Klusmeyer

Copyright © 2020 by Joann Klusmeyer.

ISBN: Softcover   978-1-950596-59-1

All rights reserved. No part of this book may be reproduced or transmitted in any form or by any means, electronic or mechanical, including photocopying, recording, or by any information storage and retrieval system without express written permission from the author, except in the case of brief quotations embodied in critical reviews and certain other non-commercial uses permitted by copyright law.

Printed in the United States of America.

To order additional copies of this book, contact:
Bookwhip
1-855-339-3589
www.bookwhip.com

1

"AMY CATHERINE, HONEY, mind you listen good. Don't you be lettin' that young fella get away. You'd best be makin' certain to get him for yerself, whilst he's still there. Mind my words, now."

Gran's voice cut into Amy's thoughts and brought her back to present reality, though it was not that she had not heard Gran's words before.

"Ain't me, Gran, that's doin' the decidin'. Johnny, hisself, seems to be in charge'a that."

"Shucks, honey, don't you be tryin' to tell me that, and me more'n sixty years older than you. Reckon I don't know when there ain't no knot bein' tied 'tween two people, them courtin' serious, that it ain't the woman at fault? Could be the woman don't want the weddin'... just thinks she does." Gran's eyes twinkled and the corner of her mouth twitched in an amused grin, her method of tempering an otherwise harsh criticism.

"But I do want a weddin', Gran, and you know I do. It'd just be that Johnny's so stubborn, there ain't no movin' 'im once he gets his mind set."

"They's ways'a takin' care of stubborn fellows," Gran assured her with a nod of the head, creating a ripple in the wrinkles from her chin to the neck of her summer dress. "When a girl gets to be sixteen, like you, she'd be old enough to be learnin' them ways. She got'a learn to know what a man gonna do 'afore he does it, so if it ain't what she wants him to do, she can keep him from doin' it. If he ain't put into words that's when the girl gets him to change his mind, he don't have to be thinkin' he'd done give in to her, and went back on his own word. Ain't no man gonna want that to happen."

Gran paused and studied Amy's face to see if she was comprehending this difficult lesson. Gran knew it was up to her, and her alone, to teach this girl the woman's way of life. At her own advanced age, Gran knew she had not much time left for the teaching.

When she noted the girl was listening, Gran continued. "Goin' back on his own words, that'd be somethin' a good man don't never want'a do. 'Course, men bein' the way they be, they find themselves sayin' 'thout thinkin', then wishin' they'd kept their mouths shut, 'cause they find themselves to be stuck with their own words."

Gran looked out beyond the worn, unpainted porch rails toward the mountaintops in the distance. She gazed there more from habit than from seeing, because her faded blue eyes no longer saw the series of mountain ranges, fading from blue, to light blue, and into sky blue, in the distance. Her strong chin was set firmly, and the soft dimple of years ago was a crowsfoot network of fine wrinkles. She thrust her hunched shoulders forward to set the creaky willow rocker into slight motion.

Amy sat on the porch step at Gran's feet, staring in the same direction as Gran, but her thoughts were on Gran's words and not the mountains. Her face was smooth and tanned, and the dimple in her chin was deep and rounded. The set of her chin, however, was a copy of Gran's, the person she had been named for. She knew Gran had more to say.

"But, Gran, Johnny done said he'd not take no wife till there was land of his own to put her on. Said it was the right thing for a man to do, not even botherin' to ask me first."

"Then why ain't he got that land? He has hisself money, ain't he?"

"Yeah, but maybe he thinks he ain't got enough. Come time he hears of some place up for sale, he goes to look. Seems like every time he has money enough, he don't like the lay of the land, or it's got no barn or somethin'. If it's a place he'd like, seems he don't have money enough. Been like that right along. Don't know rightly what I could say, him already sayin' what he said."

Gran smiled down at her, the lines of her face rearranging themselves into parallel rows at each corner of her mouth, and the laugh crinkles of her forehead and eyes deepened.

"You done made a bad mistake, Amy Catherine, honey, but it ain't one that can't be righted."

"How, Gran?"

Gran flexed her stooped shoulders slightly to settle more comfortably into the willow rocker. She massaged her swollen joints lightly with wrinkled hands, then rested her hands in her lap. For Gran, this was a moment of pure enjoyment. What could be more pleasureable for an old woman than to have her beautiful granddaughter asking for advice? What made it even better, was that the requested advice was in her own best field of expertise.

"First thing, right off, you got'a decide what kind'a man you're dealin' with. They's lots of kinds of men."

"I already know that, Gran. You told me. Johnny is a hayseed and gravel kind of a man, but I never did fully know why."

Gran smiled and nodded. "You 'member right, honey. Your Johnny would be hayseed and gravel. You wouldn't be wantin' 'im if he was feathers and chaff, 'cause then no words you ever said to 'im would have no bearin' on his life. Feathers and chaff, they got no anchor inside 'em to pull 'em down into real life. Puttin' a weight on top, the way livin' does to folks, that'd just crush the very life out'a 'im. Any job'a work they do, they don't never stay with. A regular day-in day-out job'd just pull 'em out'a shape. Nope, you don't want no feathers and chaff. Long comes a puff'a wind, and there they go. They got'a blow where they got'a blow, and there ain't no love of a woman that'd stop 'em." Gran nodded vigorously for emphasis.

"I know all that, Gran, but you were a'gonna tell me about Johnny."

"I will, I will, honey, but you got'a let me tell this my way. You got'a understand it while I still got the power to tell you. I wouldn't be wastin' no time talkin' to you, if that boy was sumac and clay."

"Sumac and clay?"

Gran nodded. "Them's two strong things, both of 'em with good stayin' power. They'd be good for some girls, but not for you, honey. That sumac and clay, they ain't to be moved, once they get set in the ground. The roots of that sumac bush gonna work into that clay, and they ain't never to be separated without breakin' 'em apart. They's men like that, solid and strong, makin' a girl feel safe, but too many troubles comin' at 'im at one time likely be the ruin of 'im. He'd come apart and not have the mind to bring hisself together, again. 'Course, troubles stayin' away, that sumac and clay'd bind together and be there till judgment day. But that ain't for you."

"Why not, Gran?"

"Good reason, girl. Yesssiiirrreee, girl, you marry a man what's sumac and clay, and he better already be what you want 'cause they ain't no changin' 'im and he gonna be just like he always was, and stay that way till the end'a time. And you, Amy Catherine, you don't know for positive yet, what it is you want, and like as not, he'd not be it."

Amy sighed a small, impatient sigh and squirmed slightly, still staring out over the blue mountain tops. Gran grinned again. It was good for her to learn patience. It was good for her to sit and wait. And learn. Also, it was a well known fact that most of a girl's best thinking was done while her mama or her Gran was delivering a lecture.

At length, Gran continued. "Then come time you get yourself a fellow made of sunshine and butterflies, you best be countin' on you takin' care'a 'im all his life, 'stead'a the other way around. He'd be a pleasure to look at and make you want to keep lookin' at 'im, but he gonna be nothin' to lean on in time'a trouble, such as comes to every person. Ain't no strength in butterflies.

"Sure, and that man, he got everyone likin' 'im, bein' that everyone likes sunshine and butterflies if they ain't got to be puttin' up with 'em day in and day out. Some women got themselves a man like that by accident, not knowin' no better. Them women learn how to manage and go on livin'. Got'a do with what you got, and that'd be the way'a life goes.

"But you got Johnny, and there'd be no resemblance 'tween the two. You got yourself a man made out'a hayseed and gravel." Gran rocked in silence, except for the squeak of the rocker. "Hayseed and gravel for you. That'd be the best, and that's what you got."

Amy sighed loudly. "No, I ain't, Gran. I ain't got nothin' and here you go talkin' on till the end'a time, when you could be tellin' me how to change Johnny's mind."

Gran nodded, reassuringly. "We gonna get there, honey, don't you worry none. I just want to go the long way, so as you'll know the road. Chance, you'd be needin' to talk to a girl'a your own, someday. Mighty important to know the kinds of men they is and what kind you got, so as to lay out the way'a your life in the best direction. Girl like you needs a fella like that Johnny, mark my words."

"Gran, how come you to say Johnny is hayseed and gravel? Sounds queer and strange."

"Don't sound queer to me. That Johnny, he's a nice boy. Him comin' here to court you don't keep him from findin' time to sit here on that step a minute and talk to me, an ugly, old woman. Mark my word, it ain't the sittin' here and talkin' that makes him nice. He could be pretendin' so he'd look good to you. That Johnny sits and talks to me 'afore he lets you know he's even here. I know it ain't 'cause he likes me. It'd be 'cause he knows you like me and he'd naturally want to be considerate of what belongs to you. Him talkin' to me is part of 'im courtin' you. It'd mean he wants to be everything to you and he ain't thinkin' of what he can get from you. If he was sunshine and butterflies, he wouldn't do nothin' if folks wasn't watchin'.

"Now, about that hayseed and gravel. The hayseed part'a Johnny means when he comes to the best time and place, that boy gonna be growin' into a big man on the inside. Them gravels gonna be the little rocks that holds him steady, so he don't get shifted about. They's gaps in amongst the gravel that's gonna let a lot of trash pass right on by, whilst he's lookin' after important things. Little things that don't amount to scat, they ain't gonna be a bother to 'im."

The morning sun had cleared the treetops and put the wide front porch into deep shade. Gran paused for several minutes, for proper emphasis. An important piece of advice was forthcoming.

"Yes, Gran?"

"You be certain that boy gets into the right place 'afore he settles in. He ain't sumac and clay, but he could be a mite hard to move on, once that hayseed bursts into sprouts. He'd be havin' the urge to stay with the crop."

"Crop?"

"Shore, honey, his crop bein' whatever it is he got it in his head to do. Reckon he ain't for sure, right now, and likely he's castin' about like a hound dog on scent, so now's the time to start workin' on 'im. Got'a see he don't be plowin' no ideas in the soil till he finds the right soil. Hear me, girl?"

"But Gran, how'd I know what'd be good for Johnny?"

"Amy Catherine, honey, don't never talk like that. You 'member King Solomon who had more women than he needed? He wrote down the rules for the best women… special women, like you. Last part'a the last chapter of Proverbs got the rules and you got'a learn 'em."

"Gran, you sayin' I got'a be what other girls don't?"

"Not a' tall. I ain't knowin' them other girls, and they ain't mine. I know you and I know God gives gifts down to people. If God don't hand much down to you, then He don't 'speck much back, but see He hands you a bunch, He gonna want a bunch back. Now, honey, you got'a bunch, and He's gonna hold you responsible for what you do with it. Might even hold me to account, well as you, come time I don't tell you what I know to be true." Gran paused for breath and the girl waited patiently.

"Amy Catherine, 'member this. They ain't no man alive gonna stand tall by hisself, with his woman hunkerin' down, afraid to stand up tall with 'im. God made Adam, and He done a good job, but Adam couldn't make it alone. That's when God was obliged to make Eve to help 'em." Gran nodded vigorously, as she watched the setting hen and her newly hatched chicks explore the grass beside the porch. "Yep, God hadda make Eve. Adam needed her. She was smarter."

"Eve was smarter? You sayin' a woman is smarter'n a man?"

"Sure thing, girl. It's right there in the Bible for everyone to see. Adam was made first, then Eve. She was made to help 'im. If Eve wasn't no smarter'n Adam, how in the tarnation could she be a help to 'im? God don't do no stupid things. If she weren't no smarter'n Adam, why bother to make 'er?"

Amy was more interested in Johnny than in Eve. Turning toward Gran, she looked into the faded blue eyes and asked, "Gran, if it you talkin', what exact words would you use to get Johnny to thinkin' straight?"

Gran hesitated, waiting for the right words to form in her mind, then she nodded, slightly.

"This here is what I'd say. I'd say, 'Johnny, I ain't likin' not bein' first in the mind of a man what wants to marry me.' That's what I'd say. Then Johnny, he'd say, 'Why, Amy Catherine, 'course you'd be first in my thinkin'. I love you more'n any other person.'

"Then I'd be sayin, 'Like a fish, you say! I ain't first and I ain't never been. First thing in your mind is that stupid rule about the land you ain't even got yet. You put that rule on yourself 'thout me agreein' to it. Then you speck me to put up with livin' by it. I ain't first in your mind, Mister Johnny, and if you'd only think on it a minute, you'd know it's true.'"

Amy grinned as she watched the twinkle in Gran's eyes and the mischievous tilt to her chin as she constructed the conversation.

"And then what?" she prompted.

"Then I'd say, 'You listen to me, Johnny, and you listen good. First thing you got'a do is tend to me, and then, together, you and me, we'll tend to that old land, the both of us likely findin' it quicker'n one of us lookin' alone. You done asked me to spend my life with you and you ain't aimin' to give me no say on whatever that'd be.' Yesssiiirrreee, that'd be what I'd say to Johnny."

"That's all?" Amy frowned, disappointed that the show was over.

"Yep, that's all. Ain't gonna be no need to say more. 'Course, if you was dealin' with a sunshine and butterflies kind of a man, you'd need to cry a little, so as he'd be sure to be listenin', but not your Johnny. That boy, he's too smart to be cried on. Tears out of a stupid girl, likely be enough to wash 'er right out'a his life."

Gran's voice changed to tenderness. "Now, honey, bring a scrap'a paper. I got me another picture I want drawed for your quilt."

"What is it, Gran?" demanded Amy, excitedly.

"Get the paper like I told you."

Amy hurried for the paper and a pencil. Since she had been no more than five or six, she and Gran had played this game. Amy had a good hand for drawing and Gran was making a memory quilt for her. It consisted of embroidered blocks, each block being a picture portraying something that was a part of Amy's life. The quilt blocks contained an embroidered picture of her swing in the oak tree, her rag doll, her toy dishes and her first school report card that contained all "A" grades.

There was the remembrance of her first biscuits (burnt) and her first cake (perfect, until she dropped it between the stove and the table). One block held the violets flowers growing by the brook and another was the pail of brown hickory nuts she and Gran would gather in the fall, when Gran could still walk in the woods. The rule was that Gran would decide on the next picture, and Amy would draw it. Her drawing ability had improved over the years, but Gran's needle and bright thread had faithfully reproduced each imperfection on the first scenes, as well as the drawings that had been more successful. Now, there was to be another block.

Amy brought the paper and plopped down on the porch at Gran's feet. Gran's snarled hands were fumbling with the clasp of her breast pin. The girl's heart pounded with excitement.

"Oh, Gran, your pin! Are you…"

"Now, youngen, settle yourself. I ain't fixin' to give you my breast pin, what's been with me every day of my life for more'n fifty years. We just gonna put its likeness on your quilt, 'cause it's something you wanted and asked for. I told you that breast pin gonna be with me, long as I got breath to breathe."

Amy was a little ashamed for jumping to a conclusion, but getting that pin was very important to her. That pin would help her keep alive the memory of their relationship after Gran left her. She'd get a pretty, plate glass case for it, and some black velvet to set it on. She'd keep it in an important place to look at whenever she was lonesome for Gran.

Gran's fumbling fingers had finally removed the heavy pin that had been fastened, sagging, to her light summer dress. She handed it to the girl.

"Make me a pictue of it, Amy Catherine, so's I can sew it into your quilt forever."

Humbled, Amy set the pin on her raised knee and put the paper beside her on the porch floor. She began the sketch in light strokes, to be darkened as she was sure they were right.

Gran's breast pin was large and square, and usually seemed to be butter yellow. Its facets were smooth, with no sharp breaks in the depth of light. Today, the color seemed to be sunshine mixed with butter and vanilla pudding. A slight movement brought out streaks of gold, like the deep yellow yolk of a summer egg.

Against each flat side of the pin was a tiny, sparkling gem, clear as the water from the spring, and surrounding it all was a filigree of golden lace that flashed like the sunbeams reflecting off a frosty window on a winter morning. Amy had never seen Gran without the pin on her dress front. When she went to church, it was there. When she walked in the woods, it was there. When she used to help Amy's mother with the canning, the pin was always there.

As she sketched the design, Amy asked, "Is this here the only pin Grandad ever got for you?"

Gran hesitated, puzzled. "Sure enough, honey. How come would he buy another one? This'n was the purtiest he could find, and if he got another one, it wouldn't be so pretty, would it? If I had two pins, why would I wear the one that wasn't the purtiest? If I didn't wear that other pin, what would be the use'a havin' it? Be no reason, I'd be thinkin'.

"'Sides," she continued, "money always bein' scarce as hen's teeth, he like as not paid more for this'n than he had ought. Goes to show you, men got times when they don't show too good'a sense."

Amy was now drawing the lacy border. "How much money did he pay for it, Gran?"

Gran lifted her eyes to look out over the blue hills. "Too much, youngen. You can bet it was too much."

The girl finished the sketch and handed the paper and the broach to Gran. Gran did not look at the sketch or the pin but held her eyes lifted toward the hills. The gnarled fingers turned the pin over and over, as if caressing every familiar detail and reliving the pleasant times of her life.

"Amy Catherine, honey, when I go, they's gonna be a surprise that I'm gonna be leavin' to you, you bein' my onliest granddaughter."

"Gran, you ain't goin' no place. I ain't ever lettin' you leave." Amy's mouth was sober and her green eyes, moist.

"Sure, and you gonna let me go. You'd not want to stop me goin' to a better place. I'm a'sayin' to you, that when I'm gone, they's a paper to be read, tellin' you about the surprise. It'll be about somethin' I want you to have, that was mine."

In a very soft, low voice, Amy asked, "The pin, Gran? That paper gonna say I get the pin?"

Gran's smile rearranged her facial wrinkles and the mischievous tilt came back to her chin as she looked down at her only grandaughter. "Now if I was to tell you what the paper said, where'd be the surprise? Tell me that? About what'll happen to this pin, that'll be knowed when the time gets here."

Amy grinned with Gran. "But you won't be gonna go nowhere for a long time, 'cause they's a lot of blocks left on my quilt and you ain't goin' nowhere till they all get filled."

Gran nodded, turning her attention to the paper in her hand. She looked at it and then at the broach in her lap.

"It seems the beatinest thing to me, how them pictures come out'a your hand lookin' just like they went into your eyes. That'd sure be one of them gifts you got from God that God's gonna speck you to make the most of."

"What's gonna be the next block, Gran?" The girl coaxed.

"Somethin' special. We fixin' to get started on somethin' extra special. Then we got that middle block for that ring that Johnny gonna give you. I got me a special idea and we gonna talk about it, time I get this block stitched."

Amy Catherine Darnell drew her knees up to her chin and hugged them with both arms, creasing her chin dimple so deeply that it disappeared. "Gran, what you said for me to tell Johnny, you for sure think it'll work?"

"Sure enough, child. No question about it."

"Gran, I just don't know how come you to know what words to say to Johnny to make him say what you want said."

"Ain't hard to do. Them may not be the exact same words Johnny'll say, but the meanin', that'll be there. I didn't marry me a man, birth him four sons, and get three of 'em raised to manhood, 'thout knowin' the way the mind of a man works."

Her eyes twinkled as she continued, "Why, the first time I set eyes on your mama, her not even bein' as old as you, I say to myself, now there'd be the girl for my littlest boy. Watched me that girl, I did, makin' note of the way she done and acted, seein' if my first sight'a her was true. I made note of the way she took on her share of the work 'thout bein' asked. Never, one time, did I see somethin' out'a her to make me change my mind.

"After I watch a while, I say to your mama, 'Essie, honey, you ever take notice of that youngest boy of mine?' And your mama, she say, 'Yes, ma'am, I take notice and I knowed he was your boy.' Then I says to her, 'Then you need to let him see you take notice, 'cause he's not nearly so quick at things as you are. He's a good boy, but sort'a blind to things important. 'Nother thing,' I says to your mama, 'me not havin' no girls to help me, come cannin' time, I could sure make good use of a bit'a help. If your mama was to see it in her heart to make me the loan'a you for a week or so, we could get a lot done, you and me.' I looked in them pretty eyes of her'n, like you got from her, and I saw that girl could rightly see what all we could get done."

Gran paused and looked full into Amy's face. Amy was grinning and her eyes sparkled. "Then what, Gran?" she prompted.

"Then your mama says, 'Sure, Miz Darnell, if you was to ask my mama, I know she'd want me to be a'helpin' you, you not havin' any girls and her havin' a'plenty to spare.'"

Gran nodded. "Amy Catherine, honey, your mama was one purty girl. They's lots of girls purty on the outside, and men bein' what they are, oft times, they don't get past that part. Your mama, now, she was purty all the way through. I done the right thing by her and me both. Your daddy needed a bunch'a help, and that girl had a lot'a help she was bound to give to someone.

"Now you go tell your mama, when the string beans need snappin', I'll be sittin' here ready. First thing, go bring me my sewin' basket."

"Sure, Gran." Amy unfolded herself and left Gran to the satisfaction of her memories. In a minute, she was back with the basket and another question.

"Gran?"

"What, honey?"

"Did you find Aunt Ellie for Uncle Arthur?"

"Sure enough did. You think your Uncle Arthur could'a found a woman like your Aunt Ellie iffen he was left to his own lookin'? Your uncle, he's a good man and he was always good to his mama, but he couldn't hardly find his own head with both hands. If he hadn't got help, there's no tellin' what he'd'a come up with and then we'd be stuck with her. He was lucky I was able to find Ellie for 'im."

"But you didn't find no one for Uncle Basil." It was a statement, not a question.

Gran's eyes clouded and she sighed. "Even the best woman ain't able to find what ain't there to find. When a man grows up to be made out'a wishes and dreams, ain't nothin' what's actual and real is ever gonna be satisfyin' to 'im. A man needin' to grab a handful'a rainbow colors, he'll likely find he got hisself an empty hand and nothin' to hang onto. Ain't no woman alive as'd be enough for that kind of a man, and I couldn't bring it on myself to let some good woman spoil her life a'tryin'. Found myself havin' to tell that to two good girls, each of 'em wantin' to love him."

Gran's voice trailed off into sad memories and Amy eased away, closing the door softly as she slipped back into the house. But she still heard Gran's voice.

"Good girls, they was, too. Right good girls…….. but I had'a let 'em go…."

2

THE LITTLE PONY was named Paintbrush because of his distinct and vibrant colors. He was splashed with gold, almost as bright as orange, his face was black, but the blaze on his forehead was white above his creamy chin and brown underbelly. His tail and mane were a shiny chocolate and each foot sported a short, white sock above his dainty, shiny hoofs. No workhorse was this one. Being so slight, he was of no use in heavy pulling. He could, however, manage the light buggy in grand style, arching his trim neck and stepping high when he had onlookers. Long ago, his name had been shortened to "Brushy" and his main duty, of late, had been to make trips up and down Five-Mile-Hill, and back and forth from Amy's house.

Today he was climbing the hill, allowing his gait to become slower and slower until Johnny Scott was obliged to encourage him with a tap of the rein on his rump and a few sharp words.

Johnny had been to Amy's house many times and now it almost seemed like his second home. He had come first as a toddler when his mother came visiting Amy's mother, and he had played with her brothers. Later, he came on his own, because of the brothers. Now, the brothers were all married and gone, and he came to court Amy.

He was somewhat discouraged this evening. He had just come from another fruitless trip to look at another piece of land. It had been a nice one with a lot of possibilities. Small but nice. There it sat, with good fences and a small house in excellent condition. It was located on the morning side of the mountain, ideal for a farmer wanting early sun in the summer and shade from the mountain in the evening. It had two everlasting springs that emptied into a good trout stream, and he had almost enough money for it. In fact, his Pa would be glad to arrange a small loan, which he could work out. But he didn't take it.

He didn't take it because it just wasn't right. He was glad he had not told Amy he was looking at another piece of land. Girls wanted explanations. They put words on things and then those things became whatever it was they called them. Not buying that farm would be called a "failure" and he didn't want any more of them.

Sure, all things had a name. Like the dread that settled in his stomach when he said "no" one more time. One thing, he knew, had to be remembered. Land was important, and when a man bought his land and moved away from his folks, it was a permanent thing. Sort of like choosing a girl to marry. A man put his thought, his time and his sweat into a piece of land, and then it was a part of him, rather like another hand. His land would have to be land that he could make use of, like another part of him. Amy, being a girl, just didn't understand what that meant.

The little pony trudged on up the stony trail at Johnny's urging, his small hoofs finding solid footing among the loose rocks. The wagon road that came up from the valley was wider and easier to travel, but the trail down into the hollow and through the woods was faster. In the winter, when the leaves fell, Johnny could see Amy's house at eye level, but the trip down into the valley between, and up again on the other side was almost a mile. He and the pony were on this trail so often he could have shut his eyes and given the pony his rein and still arrive at Amy's front gate.

Brushy followed the path around the cedars, grabbing with mobile lips at clumps of clover growing along the way. He had chomped one certain clump so many times it was now no more than a nub, still trying to regrow.

Approaching the farm from the rear, this way, Johnny came to the out-buildings in reverse order to their degree of use. First was the big storage hay barn with horse stalls at one side. Then came the goat shed. The milk cows were housed close to the goat shed, and the henhouse was a lean-to against the barn. Everything was placed for efficiency.

Closer to the house was the smoke house, hanging full of cured meat. No doubt about it, Mr. Darnell had himself a good farm here and even with five boys to help him get it started, it was a big spread. A farm this size would make a good living for a large family.

Johnny had been best friends with the youngest son, Dave, now married to Amy's best friend, Louise, and they expected a child soon. Amy Catherine, alone, was left at home, and there she stood, no more than fifty feet in front of him.

She was preparing to draw water for the patient cows. In her hand was a pitcher of water and she carefully poured the water into the bowl of the pump, working the handle in quick strokes, to soften the leather valve. A few strokes of the pump handle primed the pump, and out gushed the sparkling water.

Johnny stopped still and watched. Now that was one pretty picture! Her taffy hair blended with the taffy shade of her skin. The starched fabric of her dress puffed out the sleeves and skirt, making her waist appear to be only inches around. Certainly no larger than he could encircle with two hands. In deference to the warm weather, her hair was pulled back to the nape of her neck and tied with a stiff, white ribbon.

Johnny stroked his chin in wonderment. How could this lovely creature have evolved from the freckled, spindly-legged child with the turned up nose and missing teeth, who always clutched the worn rag doll under an elbow while playing with other toys? The doll was always there. Its wadded stuffing made curious lumps in unlikely places, creating strange, lopsided expressions on its fabric face. Seeds of motherhood must have sprouted early, because she was never seen without the doll. Until lately. Another reason for wonderment was that she might, just maybe, become his one day.

There she stood by the well curb, pumping with rhythmic strokes, totally unaware of his presence, and looking totally beautiful.

Brushy became restless and reared his head to snort at a fly, jingling his harness wildly. Amy startled at the sound and stopped pumping. The cows raised their heads, one by one, the clear, cold water drooling down their chins, dripping back into the hollow log trough.

"Johnny! You sneaked up on me."

"Didn't neither," he grinned. "Came right up the hill, like always, and you knowd I was comin' and you got all fixed up, purty. I'll just put Brushy in the corral."

The girl pumped a few more strokes as she waited for Johnny to return.

"You shore do look purty," Johnny repeated as they sat down on the curbing of the well. "You look like you didn't do a minute's work all day."

Amy grinned, accepting the compliment. "We done considerable more than a minute's work, bein' that we put up mean, old snap beans. Thought I'd never get the green off my hands. Johnny, look over here to me. Straight on. Let me see your eyes."

Johnny turned toward her as she critically studied his face.

Amy frowned. "Johnny, you went out to look at more land today, and you didn't buy it." It was a statement, not a question, and her lips were firm as she continued to study his features.

"How come you to know that?" Johnny demanded.

"Your eyes said it to me. Your mouth said it wasn't me that made you sad. Only other thing that could'a done it was that land."

Johnny's smile faded as he nodded his head slowly. "Sure, I did look at a farm. Wasn't right, though."

Amy was sadly sympathetic. "Folks wanted too much money for it?"

Johnny shook his head. "Not all together that."

"Then what?"

"Don't rightly know, thinkin' back on it. I looked at it and I wanted it, but then I didn't want it. When I put out money for land, its got'a be all 'want' and no 'don't want'. I ain't wantin' to feel no dread on it after it's done."

"But, Johnny, you thinkin' they's a place in the whole wide world that's got nothin' bad about it?"

"Reckon they's got'a be, or I got'a do a lot'a lookin'."

They sat side by side on the well curb, not looking at each other. Amy picked up Johnny's drooping hand and traced the length of each calloused finger with her own, then drew circles on his palm with her finger.

"Johnny?"

"Yeah?"

"If you had all your d'rathers in one place and all the money you needed, what kind of'a place would make you happy?"

Johnny turned to look at her. "Why'd you say that?"

"'Cause I want to know, silly. Why'd I want to waste time askin' questions if I didn't want to know the answers?"

"Oh."

There was a pause. The only sounds were the swilling of the cows with their noses in the water of the trough, and the "caup-caup" of contented hens as they scratched the grass.

"All right, Johnny Scott." Amy's voice was stern and harsh, "You start talkin to me right now. I wanna hear words comin' out'a your mouth."

Johnny sighed a long sigh and opened his mouth. Nothing came out, so he closed it, again.

"Talk to me," she demanded, mercilessly.

"Aw, Amy. I can't come right out and tell you that."

"But you're gonna. You can do it on your own, or I can drag it out'a you."

"But Amy..."

"Which way you wantin' it to be?"

Johnny looked at the toes of his shoes.

"So you made up your mind and we got'a drag it out'a you," Amy concluded. "If that'd be what you want, then here we go. Was you wantin' to get a big place, a medium sized place or a little place?"

Johnny tried to look away, but Amy's hand under his chin drew him back.

"Let me hear words, Johnny Scott."

17

"Aw, Amy, men don't be botherin' women folks with stuff like that. They just do what they got'a do, makin' up their own minds."

Amy nodded, slightly. Just like Gran said. There it was, right out in the open. He was hiding things that needed to be talked about.

Johnny signed with relief. That was over and now they could go on to pleasanter things. Amy should have known all of this without his having to tell her. She grew up in the mountains, same as he did, and she knew about the pride of the men and their feelings of responsibility toward their women. But then, here she was, three whole years younger than he was. Maybe she really didn't know, but now she did. Now she would let him alone with his problem.

"You want, let's go for a walk down the road?" he suggested, hopefully.

"Nope."

"Then what?"

"Johnny Scott, we'll be sittin' right here, come daylight, if you don't start talkin' about what I want to hear."

"Aw, Amy..."

"You wantin' land to be on the east of the mountain or the west? You want level land, bench land or maybe goat slopes? You thinkin' buildings could be there when it's bought, or are you plannin' your own?"

Johnny reached his hand toward her and she took it, placing it firmly, palm down on the cool well curb. To make sure she was understood, and that it was not an idle gesture, she placed her own hand on his and pushed down, firmly. Then she drew her hand away. She clasped her hands together in her lap and turned to look at Johnny.

Johnny was trapped. Color arose behind his sun-browned complexion, and he looked down at his hand.

"I'm still a'waitin', Johnny."

Johnny now knew for sure that he had lost. He drew in a long breath and let it out. That bought a few seconds of time but Amy's green eyes held him, relentlessly.

"Well, if I had my d'rathers, I mean, if I was to make up a piece of land to be just what I'd like, it'd be mostly level."

The girl nodded, encouragingly.

"And I'm a'thinkin' it'd not have to be big, less'n I was plannin' to buy up for sons. Rather not do that. Sons, they got 'em a right to choose for themselves. Ten acres, that'd do it. No more'n twenty. It'd need a good spring on the uphill side, lettin' water seep underground. It'd need to have high underground water, for a well."

Johnny paused and Amy waited in silence. After a minute, she encouraged him, "Doin' good, Johnny, but now ain't the time to stop."

Johnny scratched his head and flexed his shoulders, uncomfortably.

Amy weakened. "Likely you'd like to sit in the parlor? Or the porch swing? No, we can't go there. Gran's still there. I know, we'll go walkin', just you and me."

She was off the well curb in one fluid movement and she grasped Johnny's hand, urging him to his feet.

They walked past the porch. The sun was going down now and Gran could no longer see to embroider on the quilt block, so she had put it aside and had allowed her eyes and her mind to wander, peacefully, over the restful scenery of the misty blue hills. Amy and Johnny came around the house and down the walk, swinging their clasped hands between them. With his free hand, Johnny waved.

"Evenin' Miz Darnell. How you been?"

"Right tolerable, Johnny. How's your pa and ma?" Gran had asked him the same question yesterday, and they had been fine, but politeness dictated that the question be asked again.

Johnny responded, correctly. "They both doin' good, Miz Darnell. Ma's doin' some cannin' and Pa, he's tryin' to get the horses shod."

"Sure, and them things got'a be done. Tell 'em howdy for me."

"Sure thing, Miz Darnell."

By now, they were out the front gate and had started down the path toward the spring. They walked in silence past the vegetable garden, strong with the pungent smell of late marigolds blooming along the fence.

They cleared the lip of the hill, and walked into the dark shade of a bower of tall trees. Muscadine grapes filled the tops of the trees with their lush greenery and clusters of green fruit, nestling at intervals along the stems. In late September, the vine would be dotted with purple-black fruit, ready to be picked before the possums got them.

The ground around the spring had been laid solid with flat-surfaced stones and the water from the spring flowed over them as it made its way down the hill. Pale, green watercress grew between the rocks, freshened by the constantly running stream. The cold, clear water whispered across the stones, then disappeared over the lip of the hill.

One large rock jutted from the side of the mountain making a perfect bench. Amy sat down on the rock and Johnny stood beside the pool of the spring.

"Got a good spring'a water, here," he commented. "Have a spring'a water like this uphill of a garden, a body'd be havin' a real good crop."

Amy listened quietly, but Johnny had no more to say. He sat silently beside her on the rock, continuing to watch the flow of the water.

"You like this here farm, Johnny?"

"Sure. You pa done a good job, here."

"You wantin' to buy a level, hilltop farm like this'n?"

Johnny hesitated. "Rather thought it'd be not so high up the mountain. Always thought Five-Mile-Hill to be a bit out'a things."

"You sayin' you don't like bein' out'a town like this?"

"Sort'a."

"Bottom land?"

"Huh? Oh, I dunno."

"Sure you know. Say 'yes' or 'no'."

Silence. The sudden whirr of a cicada's wings punctuated the murmur of the water and the soft rustle of the overhead branches.

"Johnny?"

"Huh?"

"Now we got somethin' straight. Here's what we got. You want ten or fifteen acres of bottom land, not too far from town."

After a pause, he responded. "Now, Amy, land like that'd cost money that I ain't got and see no way'a gettin' no time soon. Time spent gettin' money is time away from us gettin' married."

"Johnny, we ain't talkin' costs, right now. We are talkin' about what you like."

"But I done figured on a hill farm to start. Then later on, we'd trade for somethin' better."

Amy watched Johnny's face as he spoke. Darkness was settling on the mountaintop and light was dim under the muscadine grapes, but she could still see the wistfulness on his face. She wanted to hold his face between her hands and say, "I love you, Johnny." Maybe she would let him kiss her. But no, she knew she would not do that because, stronger than the urge to comfort him, was the force of Gran's words. "Don't let that boy plant his crop till he gets wherever it is he wants." Amy knew the crop was not corn and beans, it was his life.

Also, it was Amy, herself, and his farm animals that he wanted. It was their children. Gran was right. Johnny was about to set his roots in the wrong place and then he'd never get away.

Darkness had almost blotted out their features. Johnny would have reached for her hand, but she quickly drew her knees up under her billowing skirt and hugged them with her arms. It was time for another approach.

"I still ain't able to decide what it is I want to be," she said.

Johnny turned to face her. She could barely see the unaccustomed frown in his forehead. "Girl, what're you sayin'? Ain't no need for you to decide what to be. You gonna be my wife."

She did not smile and she did not reach her hand toward him. She just sat there, staring toward the dark water of the spring.

Johnny tried again. "How come you to say you don't know what to be? You done promised to marry me and I'm workin' on makin' that happen."

"But that was before."

"Before what?"

"Before I knowd what you was inside."

"Now, Amy, I swear I ain't got no inklin' what you're talkin' about. You gonna tell me what's goin' on, or do I got'a be sittin' here, a'guessin'?"

Amy Catherine waited a meaningful moment. "I reckon you got a right to know about me. I got me two choices. I been thinkin' I don't know if I want to get me a job of work down at the Mercantile in River Bend. That'd be one of the things I was thinkin'."

Johnny sighed, but was otherwise silent. Her heart ached for him, but she forced her voice to be sharp. "I done found out I ain't first with you, Johnny Scott, and you'd'a knowed it too, if you'd stopped to think. First thing on your mind ain't me, 'cause all you can ever think on is that old piece'a land you're gonna get. What's more, there ain't no place on earth gonna make you happy, 'cause you ain't wantin' to hold out for the right place."

This was too much for Johnny. "Amy, how come you to be actin' like this? I said to you over and over, a man's got'a have the right place first. Then he thinks on gettin' hisself a wife. Every girl got the right to expect that out'a a man wantin' to marry her."

Whereupon Amy glared fiercely at Johnny. "And that's another thing. You make up some dumb old rule in your thick head and make yourself think it's gonna be law. You didn't give me no chance to agree or not. Then you speck me to put up with livin' by it. I ain't first in your thoughts, Mister Johnny, and you'll agree if you think on it."

"But, Amy...."

The girl was not finished. "You listen to me, Johnny Scott, and you listen good. What you need to be doin' is thinkin' 'bout how to tend to me. Then, if you do that good, we can tend to that old land, both of us, together. You think two can't find what you want quick as one, alone?

"'Sides, how come you to be a'wastin' time lookin' all over the mountainside when it's valley land you want? I don't know how you think you gonna find bottom land up there. Seems to me like you and me are strugglin' to go in at the back door, with the front door swingin' open. You got no trust in me. You ask me to spend my whole life with you and you ain't givin' me no say of where to do it. Do I deserve a say, or don't I?"

The song of the night birds had reached full pitch. The piercing call of the whippoorwill on the opposite hill echoed through the valley. An answering call came from the smokehouse by the back door. A cloudbank was building in the west and lightning cut a jagged streak through the black sky. Distant thunder followed.

Amy commented in a calm, everyday voice. "Looks like we fixin' to get a rain shower."

Johnny did not respond to the weather report. "All them words you're sayin', do they mean you changed your mind about gettin' married?"

"Johnny, I can promise you I ain't gonna marry you, like you stand. If you want to change into someone who'd think of me first, likely we could get married, like you want to."

The young man sighed. "What you want me to be? You sayin' you'd marry me without no place to put you? 'Thout a house to call yours?"

"Johnny, you got money?"

"Some."

"Then that's like havin' a part of a farm in your pocket. When you ain't spent money on that land, it means you still got it."

"Yeah, but…."

"Then when we both go to look for land in the bottoms, like you want, we'd likely find it. Ain't gonna find no valley land on the mountain and we got no time to waste a'lookin'."

"But, Amy, it'll be a long time 'afore I have me the money to outright buy ten acres of that bottom land."

"I know that, Johnny, and that'd be why I said I didn't know what it was I wanted to be, teachin' at a school or workin' at a job in River Bend. Even thought for a while of findin' someone to stay with in Jacksonville. A girl could find a job there, I'd think." Amy said no more on the subject because Gran had said that would be enough.

Johnny sighed, again. "You ain't thinkin' to help pay for the land 'cause I ain't got enough money, are you? I never wanted that."

In a soft voice, Amy responded. "Then I promise you, Johnny Scott, I'll not be helpin' you. I can make you another promise. I'll be a'helpin' someone. And if that fellow ain't gonna be you, then you need to go and leave me be, 'cause I got me a lot'a lookin' to do to find another fellow to take your place. I done spent a lot'a time on you, and I got'a be settled in with someone 'afore I get too old and ugly so as no fellow'd want me."

Large scattered drops fell whispering on the muscadine canopy but the rock ledge was still in the dry. Johnny reached for her hand.

"Come on, I got'a take you back to the house 'afore you get soaked."

She ignored the hand. "You ain't takin' me nowhere. This farm is where I live and I know every square foot of it. Reckon I can find the house 'thout no help from you. I can sit here on this rock as long as

I want and little old raindrops never hurt no one. You'd best get your pony and go, 'cause we done said 'bout everything that needs sayin'."

Johnny hesitated, looking at her, but she would not meet his gaze. Finally, he turned and walked slowly up the path, leaving her sitting on the rock. The rain had now filtered through the tree limbs and was making splat-splat sounds on the carpet of dry leaves around her. Drops fell on her head and back, and now the starched, puffed sleeves of her dress hung limply against her arms. The crisp ribbon wilted and water ran in rivulets down her face. Still she did not move. She wondered why Gran had not warned her that Johnny might just walk away.

Tears blended with the rain, washing streams down her face. The rain was now coming down full force and she was drenched. The bouncy fullness of her skirt was wilted and plastered against her legs and the rock. The rain muffled her sobs and diluted her tears and she leaned forward to bury her face in her arms.

The noise of the summer storm was so loud, Amy did not hear the sound of Johnny's footsteps running back down the path. He called her name and she looked up, startled. He took her hands and pulled her to her feet, practically dragging her up the path toward the house.

He shouted above the rain. "I ain't rightly sure what it is you want, Amy, but I got'a say, you was right to try to get it. Chances are, I need whatever help you'd want to give me. Figure I just got'a understand what it is you want."

By now they were on the front porch. Their sodden clothes dripped puddles on the unpainted floor beside the willow rocker. Amy shivered and Johnny's arm held her tight. He kissed her ear.

A beam of light shone through the window, lighting the porch and Amy shoved her hand gently against Johnny's chest. "You got'a go now, Johnny, but we got ourselves talkin' to do. Likely, we got understandin' in there somewhere. We just got'a find it."

Johnny ran to the corral for Brushy. It was a fast ride home through the rain. Johnny was soaked to the skin but the bone-wetness was no problem to him. Water could be counted on to dry out, eventually, but who could figure the mind of a woman?

Between midnight and morning, Johnny's tired mind had settled on a single premise. On dealing with women, likely it was easier to hang back and see which way they wanted to go, then encourage them to go in that direction. He'd tell Amy she could set the day. That'd give her something to aim for.

Minutes before the first rooster crow, Johnny finally dropped off to sleep.

On the opposite mountain, Amy unbuttoned her dripping dress in the darkness of the porch and draped it across Gran's willow rocker. The lamp lighted porch had returned to darkness and the sodden girl eased quietly through the front door and into her bedroom. She stood in the darkness of her room and smiled. A warm, solid feeling filled her whole body and she no longer shivered from the cold rain.

Gran was right and Johnny was the one for her. Johnny would let her help him. They would understand each other and they would work together. Yesssiiirrreee, that Johnny, he was the one for her. Then she fell into bed and was instantly asleep.

3

AMY WAS AWAKE when the barnyard roosters began their chorus. Life on the farm was difficult for a morning sleepyhead, and she was accustomed to getting out of bed early.

The storm was past and the sky was light toward the east as she swung her feet off the bed. Her underthings were still damp from last night, needing to be hung on the line to dry. She slipped into her everyday work dress and went to the kitchen. Mama was punching down the lump of light bread dough and Gran was sitting by the window, watching her. Pa came in with the pail of morning milk, which he poured through the cheesecloth strainer into the tall, shiny cream separator. The kitchen buzzed with activity.

The iron skillet sizzled with bacon and ham. Mama left the bread to rearrange the meat in the pan. Amy took the handle of the milk separator and began to turn it. Slowly at first, then gathering speed. Added to the sounds in the kitchen was the drone of machinery and now a stream of white milk appeared in the milk spout of the separator. Then, seconds later, the cream came down the other spout. She continued turning the machine until all of the milk had run through it.

Pa came in again with an armload of small sticks for the kitchen cookstove. The heat from the stove and the summer weather blended to make the kitchen very warm. Gran fanned herself lightly with the cardboard fan from the Jacksonville Funeral Parlor.

Mama pulled chunks of dough from the pan and kneaded them into small balls. When the baking pan was full of the dough balls, it was set aside to rise up into hot rolls.

A fly zoomed across in front of her mama's face.

Gran said, "Amy Catherine, honey, hand me that swatter. I'll get that nasty fly when it comes over here."

Pa came in again, and another fly came with him. He sat down at the table. "On account of that rain last night, we can't be pickin' them beans for a couple'a hours. Got'a let them vines dry."

"Splat!" went the swatter.

Now there was only one fly in the kitchen.

Mama rolled dough on the breadboard and spread it with sugar, cinnamon and butter. With skillful hands, she rolled up the dough and cut it into swirling slices. "Be no bother to me, havin' to wait for the beans. I got plenty to do till then." Mama always had plenty to do.

"Splat!" No more flies.

"Amy Catherine, honey, hang this swatter on the nail, will you?"

Mama said, "Amy, slide that kettle'a clabber milk closer to the heat. Likely that cottage cheese'll be ready to drain after we eat."

The girl looked at these routine duties with new eyes. Everything ran smoothly for mama. Nothing was ever out of place. Bread, meat and potatoes were ready at the exact same minute. Fresh radishes and onions appeared at every meal all during summer.

Amy stirred the clabber, dragging the wooden spoon across the bottom of the kettle so the milk would not scorch. Chunks of white curd clung together, swimming in the yellowish whey. Beside her, her mama broke eggs into the iron skillet.

She watched her mother stir the eggs into a smooth, creamy mass. Then, in one moment, hot biscuits appeared (golden brown), ham slices (pink and tender), and bacon (crisp and wavy). The mound of scrambled eggs was heaped on one end of the turkey platter and pan-browned potatoes on the other end. Just an everyday country breakfast. Amy had never thought, before now, how mama got everything to be perfect and come out even. How long did it take to learn to do that?

4

LATER, AMY SAT with Gran on the porch, snapping string beans into the pans in their laps. The soft "snip-snap" of the beans blended with the song of the robin and the whirring of grasshoppers.

The rain-wilted dress was now spread on the back of the porch swing. Gran grinned at the girl. "Johnny took you for a long walk and you got yourselves caught in a shower. You get a chance to talk like I told you to?"

"Sure enough, Gran."

"How did he act when you told him what you had to say?"

"Gran, so much was said I don't rightly remember everything, but it ended up with him sayin' I could have my way about whatever it was that I wanted."

Gran nodded her head, approvingly.

"Gran, you was right about the way things was fixin' to go. I know why it is that Johnny can't find no land. What he wants to get is bottom land, costin' too much money. That made him think he had to get a mountain farm so as we could get married, thinkin' to change it, later. But, Gran, I'm thinkin' that likely he'll spend his money on what he don't want and wish he had it back later."

Gran sighed. "Bottom land. That boy, he's got a good mind on 'im for bein' so young and knowin' a good thing. Your granddad and me, we got bottom land. 'Course, in them days, it could be got for no money. Just livin' on it made it yours. There was right smart of payin' in sweat and back-breakin' work, but, still and all, it was good land.

"Down on the river, it was, close to where they built the town. Water runnin' swift along side, full of trout and bull cat. Good turtle catchin', too." Gran's eyes were dreamy and her voice trailed away as she looked out over the mountaintops. A slight smile formed on her thin, wrinkled lips. For a moment, she was a bride again, living on her land by the river. Amy waited and, eventually, Gran returned.

"Your granddad was a lucky one, bein' the member of the family close by when his uncle had to take his wife back east to her people. Had him a section staked out, the uncle did, and couldn't stay to prove it up. Your granddad wasn't no older than your Johnny at the time, and he got to live there and prove it out for hisself. Too bad for his uncle but we did right by that piece'a land, your granddad and me."

The inch long sections of string beans dropped rhymatically into the pans. Amy took Gran's pan and emptied it into hers, then carried the finished product to her mother, preparing the glass jars in the kitchen.

While the girl was gone, Gran sat with her hands idle, staring past the porch rails. When she returned, the story continued.

"Built a good cabin, your granddad did, though that first one wasn't no bigger than this here porch. Big enough, though that first year with us tryin' to cut wood enough to keep warm. Bottom land is good till the winter comes, then that dampness cuts clear through hide and flesh, right into the bones. Not so bad for young folks, workin' hard. Must'a made it, though, 'cause here we sit."

Gran became aware of Amy and turned to her. "Child, you got things to say and here I go, ramblin' over thoughts long gone by. Talkin' on and on, like the old woman I got to be. I see you bein' deep in thought. Say what's on your mind."

"I got thoughts, Gran, and they sure ain't ladylike. I figure I'll be goin' out and doin' what nobody's gonna want me to do."

Now Amy had Gran's full attention. "Amy Catherine, honey, you got'a always 'member how you was brought up and how you can't be bringin' no shame on your ma and pa. You got'a open up and tell me what it is on your mind so as we can get a good look at both sides of it. An old woman like me…" Gran hesitated.

The girl nodded and sighed, loudly. "I'd like to, Gran, but it's about me and Johnny, and I ain't sure it's somethin' you'd like."

Gran responded with concern. "Still and all, honey, they's other folks to consider."

Amy nodded. "I know. I get to thinkin' 'bout things and I hear things Johnny has to say. Me, bein' past sixteen, it'd naturally be time I took myself away to my own house, but I ain't wantin' to go, just like that. I figure I got years ahead'a me makin' cheese and snappin' pans'a beans and for diaperin' babies after I get other things worked out. You talk about the wise king in Proverbs and what the best kind of a woman got to be and I ain't it. I can't be all them things. Johnny and me, we get to talkin' and I get scairt."

Gran's hands were motionless and she turned to look intensely into her granddaughter's face. "You sayin' you thinkin' of lettin' that boy get away, worryin' over things as ain't happened yet?"

"Oh, no, Gran. Johnny only knows part'a my plan and he ain't gonna like the rest when he hears it. I tried to say things to 'im and saw he wasn't likin' it so I thought to give it more time. Now that I thought more, I know I got'a go on."

Amy studied her own fingers as they nimbly broke the handful of beans into pieces and dropped them with machine-like regularity into the pan

"I aim to get me a job of work. Gran."

"You mean for cash money? Like workin' for other folks?"

"That was my thinkin'."

"Now, honey, that'll take some…"

"Gran, say I marry Johnny. First thing we start off needin' a house. Then we'd need livestock and then there'd be babies and we'd be needin' every penny he'd make to be goin' to take care of the house, the livestock, the babies and me. By then, I'd likely be too busy to do anything and maybe wouldn't care anymore if I did or if I didn't."

Gran was silent, trying to puzzle a meaning out of her grandaughter's rambling words.

"Johnny says he don't need no help takin' care'a me but there's times I think he don't rightly know how much of me there is to be took care of."

Gran was still silent, being no more enlightened than before.

The puzzled girl continued, "I see mama doin' things, bein' everywhere and never stoppin'. Always she's knowin' what to do next and how to do it. She don't cry and stomp her feet when things go wrong, because they don't never go wrong. Johnny'd have a right to expect things done right and I ain't never gonna be like my mama." She heaved a sigh and reached for another handful of beans.

"Amy Catherine, honey," Gran crooned, now that she had gotten the gist of the problem. "You just 'member that no two women'd be alike, no more'n no two men. Problems looks big to you now, but they come on easy like, till you get the feel of 'em. Johnny won't speck to have biscuits like his mama cooks, 'cause he'd not be with his mama no more."

Amy interrupted, "It ain't biscuits that's a bother to me right now, Gran. I want to make cash money. I thought and thought and that's what I want. Is there somethin' wrong with that?"

"All depends," Gran qualified. "Reckon the first thing to be talkin' on is how you plan on earnin' that money."

The girl was ready with the answer."I got me two thoughts on that, Gran. One of 'em bein' to get me the books I need to study for a certificate to teach school. The other thing is to work at the Mercantile in River Bend, helpin' ladies find what they want to buy."

Gran was quiet again. It was not often she had two very important thoughts to consider at the same time, and she had a little trouble grappling with both of them, but she must try.

"Be there a place close by where you could teach? You go over to Piney or some place and not be takin' Johnny with you, that'd leave him open to some other girl what ain't got herself ideas of earnin' cash money. Chances are, Johnny wouldn't be easy to take along, just 'cause you got it in your mind to go."

"I know that, Gran, so it made me put my mind on the other thought."

"Child, you gonna run into problems, there. Have you done been asked to work? Does Mr. Jenkins say women with money was havin' trouble findin' things to buy?"

Amy grinned. "Gran, I got me an idea on that. I ain't never seen no woman down there sellin' things, but I seen a sight'a women come in to buy. They put on a pair of them new boots and look down, wonderin' how they look and how some other woman would think they look. That's when I'd go up to 'em and say, 'Howdy, Miz So and So. Nice day.' Then she'd say, 'Thought I might want to buy these boots, but I changed my mind.' That'd be when I'd say, 'Oh, yes, Miz So and So, them boots make your feet look so purty your man'd want to hold back your skirts to see 'em better. He'd likely be shamin' you in public. You'd be right not to buy them boots.' Then Miz So and So likely be walkin' plum over me, tryin' to get to Mr. Jenkins to pay her money for them boots 'afore some other woman could get at 'em."

Gran grinned, chuckling softly. Then she began to laugh. She laughed until tears streamed down her face and she began to cough and choke, causing Amy to jump up and begin to pound her on the back.

Amy's mama came running through the door, shouting, "Gran, what's wrong?"

Gran could talk, now. "Essie, honey, don't you get excited. This girl, she's amusin' her old Gran, a'tellin' stories, so as the work'd go easier. She said funny things, as got me to laughin' all the breath out'a me. I'm fine, now, Essie, honey. You got things to be doin' 'thout havin' to see after me. I'm good as new." Essie looked doubtful but the work in the kitchen was calling, so she left them.

Gran's eyes were twinkling. "It sure looked funny in my mind, seein' Miz So and So walkin' all over you, anxious to get rid'a her money."

Amy was grinning, too. "That weren't all my story, Gran. I had more I was gonna say to Miz So and So. I'd say, 'Miz So and So, I'd be obliged to let you have them boots but the truth is, I can't.'

"Then I'd pick up this here piece of yard goods, bein' of a color to go with them boots, and I'd say, 'Them boots and this here yard goods, they got'a go to the same person, on account of the way they was made to go together.'

"Then Miz So and So, she'd dig a little deeper and find money to pay the price for both of them things. She'd be leavin' that store happy and tellin' everyone she seen, "See, I got me these boots and this yard goods special 'cause they go together. That's the newest fashion, not to buy one 'thout the other.'"

Gran was chuckling, snap beans forgotten. Amy's pan was filling fast and she grinned with pleasure over Gran's enjoyment. Gran purely loved a good story.

"They'd be one more thing, Gran. When Miz So and So's friends come in, I'd pick up one of them shiny breast pins and hold it next to a piece of yard goods and say, 'Notice how this here breast pin picks up the colors out'a that yard goods? I was thinkin' I might just put this here pin back and when I got enough money, I'd be buyin' it for myself.'

"Then that woman's say, 'How much money is that breast pin? 'Cause my man, he'll be wantin' to buy me somethin' special for my birthday.' And I'd say the price to her, but I'd say it won't be still here on her birthday, 'cause I'd have my money to buy it tomorrow. Don't you reckon she'd find the money to buy it right then?"

Amy looked at Gran, waiting for her comment. She was not disappointed.

"Youngen, I think you could maybe do just what you said."

"Reckon I could."

"And, honey," Gran continued, "You ain't gonna know how relieved you made me, hearin' you say them things, and not sayin' somethin' that'd shame your family. Couldn't hardly put my mind to what you might be thinkin' on doin'. Times, I think just like a foolish old woman. That was a good story you told about Miz So and So.

"Gran, you thought any more on me gettin' a certificate to teach school?"

"Fact is, child, I thought and thought. Both of them ideas of yours got good things to be said on 'em. It come down to maybe the good thoughts be mostly leanin' to a job in a store, on account'a bein' closer, not more'n five miles away.

"Then again, I consider you'd be special good at teachin' little folks, you bein' so good at books, yourself. The thing is, seein' you go off to Piney or some other valley, that'd be kind'a mixin' up the plans and dreams I got about you." Gran sighed and closed her eyes to rest them.

"What you plannin' on, Gran? What's that got to do with Johnny and me and what I got'a do?"

"Amy Catherine, honey, don't fret yourself. I just sit here thinkin' old woman's thoughts, most of 'em likely makin' no sense. I just sit here thinkin' on the pleasure'a havin' my onliest granddaughter close by, so as to lay eyes on her from time to time, 'thout her bein' in some other valley not even bein' home to go to the church house of a Sunday. But you got no call to be thinkin' on that. Young folks got'a do what young folks got'a do, and the doin' be hard enough, 'thout old folks a'harpin' at 'em."

"Now, Gran, I ain't thinkin' 'bout what you say bein' a bother. It was me that asked you what you thought and I still want you to have your say."

Gran nodded. "Got'a put more thought into it. I got somethin' else to say that I been thinkin' on. I figure, you and me, we might be settin' together them quilt blocks, them as we got finished. It'd be somethin' you could be helpin' with. Then we gonna put on them verses from Proverbs about the best woman, and 'broider up reminders on the rest of the blocks. That there last chapter tells about it in them last verses. Seems like the wise old man was savin' up his best advice for his last words."

"But, Gram, them verses ain't a part of my life, yet. We need to be waitin' years till you know for sure if I can be that kind of a woman."

"No, child, listen to me. I ain't got years to wait. We got'a do this while I can be here. I got no doubt'a you bein' the right kind of a woman, so we gonna get that old quilt done, just like I say."

"But, Gran…"

"Got no time for arguin'. Now the first picture I want drawed is a pasture land with a river goin' by."

"But, Gran, what do I have to do with a cow pasture and a river?"

"Well, you 'member that verse that say, 'she go out and look at a field to see if it'd be worth her money and if it's a good one, then she'd buy it.'? That picture gonna match that verse. Come time we get these old beans snapped up, you gonna make that picture and we gonna get started."

Amy was still puzzled. "But, Gran, Johnny and me, we don't have that river bottom land and may not never have the money to get it."

Gran grinned. "You gonna have it, all right. Time you sell all that yard goods and all them boots, you gonna have piles'a money. You gonna have that land, child, so you just keep doin' what the wise king said to do."

Amy sighed, doubtfully. "I reckon I believe what you say, Gran. It's hard to think on, but them other things you said come true. Here, let me dump up your beans and take 'em in to mama."

While she was gone, Gran's old fingers rested on her lap. Strength in the gnarled old knuckles must be saved for the stitches required to finish the quilt. It must be finished on time and every stitch of the embroidery by her own hand, else how could she continue to offer her guiding hand after she had to leave her? She rubbed one aching hand against the other. Thin, dry skin whispered against itself like the delicate paper of the Book containing the words of the wise king. Calcified joints of her fingers bulged like knots in a strand of rope.

The morning sun had climbed above the row of trees. Gran extended her feet slightly to absorb the last of the warm rays on her toes, which always seemed to be cold.

Amy came back and sat in the porch swing, filling her lap with beans to be snapped.

"Gran, did you hate awfully bad to leave your river bottom land?"

"Truth is, honey, I did. But bein' a lone woman like I was, when granddad passed on, there weren't much choice of things to do 'cept sell it off. It brought right smart of money, too, me havin' no idea what bottom land'd bring. Gave me cash money in my hand, more'n I ever seen 'afore. Had to put some hard thoughts on how to make the best use of it.

"Had me the pleasure of buyin' them white faced cows your pa wanted and seein' 'im make herds for all his boys. Felt like it was right to do, me stayin' here, livin' off him. Always made me feel good, liftin' my own weight, times I had the chance.

"Had me money to hand a weddin' gift to your brothers and all Uncle Arthur's boys, they got somethin', too. Thought in my mind it'd be a good thing for a man to have cash money to buy his bride some little thing she wanted. Furnishin' the money made it feel almost like it was from me, too."

Gran massaged her hands, string beans forgotten as she gazed over the porch rail at the row of yellow flowers. The girl snapped beans and watched her Gran's face, sadness clutching at her stomach as she noted the strange, faraway look of it. Almost a longing, it seemed like.

5

IT WAS LATE afternoon and Brushy slowed from a trot to an amble and veered to the roadside to crop a tender clump of grass. Johnny beckoned him back on the road by a tug on the rein. Down hill was easy rolling, and Brushy trotted between the ruts of the hardened red clay, making the light buggy bounce merrily along. The occupants of the buggy were forced to grab for side handles and hang on tight, or be tossed about.

The sun was sinking behind the oaks and wild chestnuts that shaded the road, the buggy and the little paint pony. By the time they reached River Bend, five miles away, the sun would be set and Mr. Jenkins, owner of the Mercantile, would be closing his store for the day. Mr. Markham, who ran the pharmacy, would still be open for business. He would sell a dimes worth of candy at ten pieces for a penny, and Josie and Johnny would eat the candy during the leisurely climb back up Five-Mile-Hill. For certain, there would be several pieces of peppermint left in the sack for Gran.

It was dusky dark by the time the pony reached the foot of Five-Mile-Hill once more. The new moon furnished very little light, so it was necessary for Johnny to light his kerosene buggy lamps which hung on either side of the buggy high up over the wheels. The pools of light enabled the pony to see the road.

Woodland animals stopped in their prowling to watch the buggy go by, their eyes being pairs of shiny dots of reflected light. As the buggy approached, some turned and ran into the woods but some stared until the strange, noisy animal on the road had gone his way.

Brushy knew the way home and Johnny was in no hurry. So far this evening, the girl beside had said nothing of last night's conversation. She bounced along, contentedly chewing orange gumdrops and sucking peppermint sticks.

Johnny waited as long as he could. "You thought any more on when you want to get married?"

"Been thinkin' quite a lot," came the answer.

The buggy crunched in the gravel and the pony's feet plodded on, one step after the other, climbing slowly.

"Well, you thought up a day, yet?"

"I don't hardly have the day in my mind. It'd have to be after Christmas."

"After Christmas? Way you was talkin', I allowed you was in a hurry."

Amy sucked peppermint in exasperating silence for two full minutes. "I didn't say nothin' about bein' in a hurry. Seemed like I wanted a day to be set, us agreein' on it, so as I'd know what to count on. I got a sight of things I got'a get done 'afore that time gets here."

"What you gonna do, takin' so long? Sew you some new things?"

"Nope. Ain't gonna have no time for that."

"Your mama got things you got'a do at your house?"

"Nope."

Johnny's good humor was becoming frayed. "Then what things you gonna do, takin' all that time?"

"Now Johnny, you got no call to be gettin' huffy with me. I was fixin' to tell you 'cause I'll be needin' your help. First day you got that rain keeps you out'a the field, I want you and me to make a trip over to Jacksonville. They got a store over there with books like I got'a have to get my certificate to teach school."

It was now Johnny's turn to be silent as his mind grappled with Amy's strange, new ideas. How did such wild thoughts get themselves hatched in that pretty little head of hers? Married girls didn't teach school. She knew that! They didn't have to. Here she was planning marriage and still willing to put herself through the rigors of study for no known reason. Nothing was more of a puzzle than the mind of a woman.

"How come you to know about the books in Jacksonville?" he demanded.

"'Member, I told you. When I passed out'a Mr. Campbell's school, he says to me, 'Amy, you bein' quick to learn, you might think on goin' to higher grades.' I told him, 'I can't 'cause there ain't no higher school here for me to go to.'"

The crunch of the wagon wheels on the hard clay road did not drown the sadness from her voice. She went on.

"So that's when he said it me, 'Well, if you can't go to school no more, least ways you could go to Jacksonville and buy yourself the books. Reckon just everybody couldn't study by themselves, 'thout a teacher to help out, but you could.' Then he told me to take the test for a teaching certificate. Don't too many pass that test less'n they been through the seventh and eighth grades. But he reckoned if I study on my own, I could do it. Been wantin' to, off and on, ever since he said it. Gonna do it, now."

A small herd of deer stood in the road, watching the horse and buggy approach them. They considered themselves invisable in the darkness but the pairs of shinning eyes at various heights gave them away. Deer were nothing special to Brushy, who plodded on. At twenty feet, the herd turned on lightening feet and disappeared within seconds. Brushy snorted his disdain, jingling the tiny bells on his harness.

A fat, unwieldy June bug, aiming for the lamp, crashed against the buggy seat and climbed with tiny claw feet into the girl's lap. After pausing a moment, it spread its wings and aimed once more for the buggy lamp, buzzing noisily.

Amy continued in a low voice. "Anybody what can add and take away can see I got me two more year's worth'a studyin' ahead of me. It gives me weary thoughts, thinkin' of all that studyin' and not havin' a teacher to help out."

Johnny reached for another piece of candy. "For the life of me, Amy, I can't see how it'd be a pain to you not havin' more'n six years of schoolin'. It ain't botherin' me none. Fact is, goin' when I did didn't seem to do me no good. Find myself glad enough to have it behind me."

"Oh, Johnny, just think on it. Things you want ain't likely gonna take book learnin' and you done been to school a'plenty for that, knowin' how to read and write, and all. It ain't the same with me. I get this feelin' that keeps comin' back that says I could be gettin' ready to teach school."

Johnny logically asked, "You been hearin' of Mr. Wilson, that's got the job now, quittin his school? 'Cause if you ain't, he probably gonna be there a long spell'a time yet, bein' so young."

Amy was quick to respond. "My feelin' got nothin' to do with Mr. Wilson. It's all inside of me. Seems like a girl'd need to look ahead, happen the time come she'd be alone. That'd be a way to make her own way, havin' somethin' more'n the ability to cook and care for some other family. Seems like it'd be like havin' somethin' hidin' your pocket, happen you need it."

The fat, June bug rammed its body against the top of the buggy and tumbled into Amy's hair. She pinched the insect between her thumb and forefinger and pitched it out into the darkness of the road. A slim, pointed moon was rising from behind the screen of trees, but it furnished very little light. It was clearly a lover's moon.

Amy Catherine felt into the paper bag and counted six pieces of candy left. She took one and popped it into her mouth, then twisted the top of the sack and pushed it to the far side of the seat from her. She edged a little closer to Johnny and took his hand. She pulled his hand into her lap but he extracted the hand and raised his arm to lay on the buggy seat behind her back. She scooted away a bare inch and retrieved the hand. They were still three miles from home.

"Johnny?"

"Yeah?"

"If you had all your d'rathers, and didn't have to think of money or people, what is it you think you'd be doin' with your life?"

"I don't go thinkin' on things like that, Amy, 'cause there is money and there are people. You know that, well as I do, you bein' the thinkin' person of us two."

Amy retorted, "You're lyin' to me, Johnny Scott. I know you too good to be believin' that. You go walkin' 'hind that plow, droppin' bean seeds or rakin' up hay, you go to thinkin' and thinkin' on this and that. Thinkin' on dirt and seeds and if its gonna rain… and that don't take up a whole day. I know a heap'a thinkin' goes on in your head."

"Well," Johnny hedged. Apparently, this would be a continuation of last night's interrogation. He had hoped for an easier night, fearing his sanity would not hold up under another onslaught. If he could determine quickly what she wanted to hear, and say it, they might still enjoy the ride. "Well, I…"

"That's a good start, Johnny."

"Sure I do thinkin'. Every man does." It seemed as though that exasperating girl just took his whole mind into hers, shaking it like a hound pup shakes a rag mop, tearing it to shreds.

Amy released his hand and sat rigidly in the buggy seat, pulling her knees up under her dress. She turned to face him. "Johnny Scott, you gonna answer my question like I put it to you or do I got'a drag it out'a you? I can do whatever you want done, so you just tell me so's we can get on with it."

Johnny took the rein in both hands and stared ahead into the darkness.

The determined girl continued, "What it was I asked, happen you forgot, was what you think you'd like if you had all the wishes you wanted and no worries."

Johnny ran his fingers through his hair and stroked his chin. "Now, Amy, I don't be talkin' about things as ain't gonna happen. Sayin' things out loud makes 'em sound real, then when a body can't get his hands on 'em, seems like he lost something he never had. It makes a pain that don't go away. Things that don't get thought on, a body can push away and go on enjoyin' what he's got."

Amy thought about that. He had a definite grain of logic, all right. Still, when a body reached out for something, he needed to be thinking on what he'd rather have in his hand, just in case he had a choice.

"Johnny, I got'a know. I can see what you say about not givin' yourself dissatisfaction, but you and me, we talkin' about bein' with one another for the rest of our lives. I don't even know what you got inside you, less'n you tell me. All my life I look at you, comin' to our house, hollerin' across the hills to my brothers, goin' huntin' and fishin' with Dave and Willie. I saw you then, but that's all I really know about you. You got'a tell me about thoughts and wishes."

Brushy snorted and shied at the June bug. They were two and a half miles from home and there was silence in the buggy.

Amy prompted, "I know you been saving' your money for us to get a good start, and that'd be important to me. Past that, I don't know nothin'."

The buggy reached the top of the climb and was leveling out on the bench land. There was one more climb before they reached the Darnell house.

"You can start talkin', now, Johnny, 'cause I'm gonna shut up and listen."

"But, Amy, it sounds silly when a man puts into words what ain't gonna come true. I don't like you a'makin' me do this."

But the girl was merciless. "Keep talkin', Johnny. It don't matter to me, hearin' silly words."

Johnny sighed. "Reckon I got to do it. If I had what I think this minute I'd want, it would be to get a place to grow special things. I'd want it to be bottom land with deep, black soil, not like the mountain land where rainstorms beat on it and wash it away. Wouldn't want much land, 'cause good bottom land like that'd be, it goes to weeds and sprouts if it ain't watched. It'd get willows and sycamores shootin' up ten feet over night."

Johnny paused, choosing his words carefully.

Amy asked. "What kind of special things was you thinkin' on growin'?"

"Never did clearly pin it down, but it'd be regular things like pumpkins and melons, and really red tomatoes. Maybe some eggplant, and, 'course there'd be sweet taters, all orange inside, not yellow like grows on the hill. They'd be bigger and taste better, too."

Amy had been studying Johnny's face in the dim reflection of the buggy lamps. She noticed his slight grin of amusement at the suggestion that his vegetables would be better than those grown by others. She had to grin, too, but Johnny didn't see her grin or the twinkles in her eyes.

"What else?" she encouraged, reaching for his hand.

"Well, I'd be havin' me all them things and they'd be watered from underground. I'd needin' me a never-failin' spring up from the garden spot. I'd get hollow canes and fix 'em together to make water run through and go wherever I needed it. That'a'way, the heat of August'd be nothin' to them plants, them thinkin' it was spring all year long." Johnny chuckled at the ridiculousness of the whole conversation, but as long as he had been trapped into talking, he may as well make it good.

"Johnny, how do you know them plants'd grow so good? Seems it'd take more'n water."

He nodded agreeably. "I ain't thought it out clear, yet, but I been lookin' at the ground back of your pa's hay barn where he throwed out his old hay. Weeds higher'n my head come out'a that pile. Old tomato plant that got in that dirt growed 20 feet long and got tomatoes on it one end to t'other. Them plants didn't get no extra water, neither. Seems like old hay makes black dirt. Never worked it out, actual, but it's in my mind the same thing'd work on pumpkins and taters, same as hay and grass. Told pa 'bout it but he said our taters were good enough like they was. Likely, he was right."

"Johnny, I swear you been doin' a lot of thinkin' while lookin' down at the ground. Seems it'd take a lot'a jars to put all you'd raise. How many youngens you thinkin' on havin'?"

Johnny grinned. "Ain't thought that far. Sort'a figured you had that all thought out."

She shook her head rapidly. "Ain't up to me, Johnny. I figure you'd probably be smarter'n me on that. You'd know the size of a family you could take care of."

Johnny nodded. "Wouldn't need youngens to eat everything we'd raise. Thought my place'd be where people go by and see that I got. Or likely there'd be a town close by. They'd see that what I grow would be a sight better than anything they could grow, so why should they bother? I could put me a stand out on the road with my best things and a boy or two to watch. Folks'd stop and have a look and then talk about it, later. Might have on a load on my wagon of my best tomatoes, and have to run the wagon down to the livery stable for harness oil. Fellows'd scratch their heads and say why work in the heat to grow tomatoes when they could buy mine."

He paused to sigh and stare dreamily out the side of the buggy into the darkness. "Then a year or so on down the line, happen I'd be walkin' through the town and a woman on the street that heard about me, she'd say to me. 'Mr. Scott, you gonna be havin' them purple hull peas comin' ripe?' And I'd say, ' Purty soon and I'll let you know.' Then she'd likely say, 'And you be sure to 'member me when you dig out them big sweet taters, like you done last year. I want some of them.'

"'Bout that time, I'd be takin' this here little notebook out'a my pocket and I'd write down her name and what it was she wanted. Time come them things was ripe, I'd look in my book and first names'd be gettin' first choice.

"Why, I'd even put them purple hull peas in the buggy and take 'em over to her house. Or maybe send a youngen. With her not havin' to come out to the field, likely she'd be ready to pay a little more money.

"Good black land like I'd have, that'd grow as much to the acre than pa's farm gonna do in two acres. Maybe more. Leastways, that's what I figure. My apples and taters, they'd be so big there'd be hardly no peelin' waste."

Johnny paused for breath. A moth flew against his face and he brushed it away. He put his arm on the back of the buggy seat behind Amy and she did not retrieve it. They were only a half a mile from home.

Surprisingly, Johnny continued. "Ya see, I don't have no need'a eight years'a schoolin' to write down the names of folks and what they want to buy, nor to add up that it'd take less time to grow ten bushels'a roastin' ear sweet corn than twenty bushels. Goin' to school 'nuther year wouldn't make my back no stronger and readin' 'nuther book wouldn't make the sun no cooler on my head."

Johnny sighed a long sigh. This had been a very lengthy speech for him and likely he had said enough to Amy to keep her mouth shut all the way to her house.

He reached out his arm and pulled her gently against his shoulder, but it was hard to cuddle a girl who was sitting on her knees, staring at him. He pulled back his arm. They had reached the top of the hill and he could see the lights of her house shining square and yellow in the distance.

Amy watched the road ahead of Brushy's flowing mane and saw the lights of her home. With the suddenness of a hummingbird entering flower, she put her feet on the buggy floor and moved two inches toward Johnny. She reached up to the hand attached to the arm behind her back and pulled it around her. Johnny's calloused hand was warm in both of hers.

Johnny smiled to himself. He had been right. All those words of his had shut her up and here she was, holding his hand and smelling of meadow grass and peppermint. Getting along with women might be a difficult process, but at least it was possible. Eventually. Brushy turned at the drive leading to the Darnell farm. He sauntered to the yard gate and turned to look back at his passengers.

"Johnny?"

"Yeah?"

"All them things you just said, they gonna come true."

Johnny chuckled, "I said 'em good. Made you believe all them things, didn't I?"

"Sure did, and they was the truth."

"How'd you know?"

"Easy. You couldn't lie that good if you had to, Johnny Scott! Mark my words, I'll get that paper to teach school and you'll be gettin' that special garden."

Johnny sighed. "Sayin' things don't make 'em happen, but I reckon we can get you that teachin' paper. It'd take too much money to get that farm." At least there was some success.

"What'd you mean, 'we'd' get that teachin' paper? All you got'a do is take me to the bookstore. I'm gonna be the one to get it."

Johnny took Amy's shoulders in both his hands and turned her squarely toward him. "Now lookie here, Miss Amy Catherine Darnell, you ain't the only one what can lay out words on what's gonna be done. We gonna go to Jacksonville and we gonna get them books. Whatever money they want for 'em, I'll be layin' it down."

"But, Johnny, your money's for land. My pa'll get me them books."

"No." Johnny was surprisingly forceful. "You ain't gonna belong to your pa very much longer, so them books'd be rightly my cost. You ain't the only one to say what's right for you and me. You gonna be mine and it'll be me as pays for what goes into you, be it food or words. You hear that, Miss Amy Darnell?"

Johnny shook her playfully, making her giggle. She kissed his chin with a quick peck and, grabbing the candy sack, turned and jumped to the ground.

Johnny watched as she ran across the dewy grass to her porch. She waved and slipped through the door and Johnny picked up the reins and spoke to Brushy. The squares of yellow light in the farmhouse windows became black and Brushy circled the driveway and sauntered to the road. Johnny sat back and let the pony decide his own speed. He had no idea how much the books would cost, but he jogged along contentedly, certain that he had gotten his money's worth.

6

BREAKFAST WAS OVER and Gran had taken her place in the willow rocker with her slippered feet extended into the warm morning sun.

Amy's mother had taken her aside. "Amy, honey, I ain't wantin' Gran to help peel these peaches we fixin' to put up, today. Gran don't need to be leanin' over that pan like she would so's the juice don't get everywhere, makin' it hard for her to catch her breath. Top'a that, her hands ain't in no shape to be holdin' a sharp knife very long. I got somethin' I want you to do."

"What's that, mama?"

"I want you to say, 'Gran, you got'a do me a favor. I'll be workin' double fast to peel these peaches for both of us if you'll be workin' on my quilt.' Gran'll likely listen to you, her bein' partial to you. That'a'way she'd not be feelin' bad, thinkin' she ought'a be helpin' with the peelin'."

Mama grinned and patted her daughter's arm. Amy grinned back and took only one peeling pan to the front porch.

Gran agreed, reluctantly. "But I can't see how it'd be right, me sittin' here doin' needle work and your mama out in the hot kitchen, a'cannin'. Reckon I ain't as fast as I once't was, but I ain't helpless, neither."

"Don't you worry, Gran. Mama said just me peelin' was fast enough, no more'n we got to do, today. 'Sides, I'm more'n anxious to see that block finished." That ought to get Gran's mind off the peaches, she thought.

Gran smiled. "This here block with that shiny thread be comin' out real purty. Had me a thought about that middle block, too."

"But, Gran, that middle lock is for the ring Johnny'll get me. We don't know exactly how it'll look yet."

"I know, child, but I had me another thought. Somethin' else goes in that middle block. You gonna draw me a yellow daisy for the way you put me in mind'a that flower."

"You sayin' I'm like a daisy flower?"

"Some ways you are. Them yellow daisies grow up tall and when a hail storm bends 'em down, the sunshine pulls 'em right back up. Them flowers can be picked and brung in the house and they don't fade out. Pull all the flowers off the plant and it makes just as many more. Come winter, it looks to be dead but it's just hidin' in the ground. Come springtime, right there it is again, purtier than it ever was."

Amy slipped the knife through the fuzzy skin of the peach, dividing it in half. She flicked the seed into one pail at her feet and expertly sliced off the skin in another. The peeled half of the juicy fruit was tossed into her pan. The pile of halves mounted fast.

The door opened and mama brought out an empty pan and took away the full one. Gran watched.

"Now, Essie, you could let me help her. It'd be faster."

"Oh, no, Gran. I can't hardly keep ahead of this youngen as it is, me with a dozen other things to do along with cannin'. 'Member how fast them peach halves can turn dark if they ain't packed right away?" The daughter-in-law smiled brightly and disappeared into the house.

Amy resumed the conversation. "Gran, I'm not like them things you said about the daisy flower."

"Amy Catherine, child, you see yourself from the inside and likely you ain't seein' the resemblance. Folks lookin' on the outside know better what they see. 'Sides, come time you get to be what you're gonna be, the resemblance gonna be plain, even to your eyes. There ain't gonna be nothin' that happens gonna tear you down and keep you there."

In one sudden motion, the girl set down the pan of peaches and disappeared into the house. Her quickness startled Gran and she turned to stare at the door. In a few seconds, the girl was back with a small, brown paper bag in her hand.

"Johnny got us some candy. I almost forgot to give you yours."

Gran smiled at the sight of the peppermint. "That Johnny, he sure do know how to treat a girl, don't he?"

Gran sucked the peppermint, increasing the winkles in her sunken cheeks and crinkling her eyes in the enjoyment of the sweet.

"Gran, you thought any more on them things I asked you?"

"Truth of the matter is, I was a'thinkin' on them very things and I says to myself, 'Like as not, that child has done figured out what was best to be done,' so I put my mind to the finishin' of this here quilt."

Then Gran continued, "Been thinkin' to have you make me a picture of a window of a house, showin' the moon and stars outside, that bein' to represent what the wise king said about the best woman gettin' up early before daylight to make sure things got done. 'Cause if she didn't, they wouldn't. Yesssiiirrreee, I want that one.

"Then I recollect that a verse says somethin' about a woman keepin' herself healthy and strong, and her family, too, like as not. I thought up an apple for that block, bein' a thing to be eatin' for health. A red apple, it'd be, like your pa grows down on the benchland. Yesssiiirrreee, a woman puny and got no strength, she got herself a problem that's got no answer for it." The old woman nodded in agreement with herself.

"Now them's two of the blocks I got thought out and they's a sight more to go."

Gran transferred the peppermint from one side of her mouth to the other, savoring the sharp flavor. "Yesssiiirrreee, child, they's a sight more of them blocks to go. That wise king had a lot to say."

The girl waited a respectful length of time before she told Gran, "You'd be kind'a right when you figured out that I done decided what I got'a do. Done told Johnny and he took to it, right off. Still got more thinkin' to be done, though."

"What was it you done told Johnny?"

"I told 'im he'd have to be takin' me to Jacksonville, me havin' to get them books. I didn't say nothin' 'bout the cost of 'em, 'cause pa done said he'd hand me the money.

"Johnny agreed right off to goin' over there. Said he 'speck to have to pay for them books, bein' he was gonna be responsible for what goes into me, mouth or head. Likely, I best make him sit down to hear the cost, so's he don't fall down right there in the store. Near as I can guess, them books'll cost more'n a acre'a hill land."

Gran grinned and reached for another peppermint. "Like as not it'll be a shock to 'im." Then her face became serious. "You thinkin' that'd be the best plan, child? That'd mean you'd go off to some other place and not see your ma and pa."

"Can't be for sure, Gran. But there'd be nothin' happenin' no time soon. Take a person, maybe, even two years to learn them books in school. No tellin' how long it'd take me without no teacher."

Gran nodded, comforted. Two years was a long time, and for one the age of Gran, it could be forever. "Get this cannin' season over and you'll have time, a'plenty, sittin' here while I finish this here quilt."

Amy nodded her head, tempted to let the subject drop while Gran was comforted, but she had always been honest with Gran, and Gran had always understood.

"Chances are I'll be havin' to study just whenever I can. 'Member us talkin' about the job down at the Mercantile? About me sellin' boots and yard goods? Well, I still got me that idea and it keeps workin' itself around in my mind."

Gran sighed, heavily. "Amy Catherine, honey, was you meanin' all them things you said? I was thinkin' of you makin' up stories to amuse an old woman, like when you was a little tot. Is old Mr. Jenkins agreein' to it? Wouldn't think he'd be wantin' a woman messin' around in his store."

Amy chuckled. "Mr. Jenkins don't know what I been thinkin'. Reckon I'll be doin' some tall talkin' and maybe have to be a mite pushy to get it done. Gran, you 'member about the special woman sellin' girdles and things in the market? Well, this'd be kind'a like that, don't you think?"

Gran took a few more stitches. It was enough to make a body thoughtful. Was her carefully worked out plan doubling back on her? She had been explaining the verses to Amy, and now the girl was interpreting them back.

"Your mama know about this?"

Amy nodded. "Mama said she never heard of no one ever pushin' their way in, in the way I was fixin' to try, but likely if it could be done I'd be the one to do it. But pa, he don't say nothin' neither way. Heard 'im tell mama if it was one of the boys, he'd be ready to say, one way or the other. Bein' it was me, he'd just keep quiet. Said he didn't know nothin' about women folks."

Gran nodded. "Now, honey, he said the truth on that. If it weren't for me findin' your mama for him, neither you nor them boys'd be here to hear me a'talkin'."

Amy grinned, warming up to her subject. "I been practicin' how to put my hair up, and sometimes it stays as long as a minute. I got me two dresses with hems big enough to let down and two others needin' a ruffle to make 'em do. That'd be dresses enough to start."

Gran pointed out, "Now if you was to talk Old Mr. Jenkins into goin' along with this, you still got five miles down there and five miles back. Johnny ain't gonna be free to take you on account he got work to do. Does Johnny know about this?"

The screen door opened and mama came with an empty pan in exchange for the full one.

Gran looked up from the embroidery. "Essie, honey, you right sure you don't want me to be workin' on them peaches? It'd get 'em over faster for you."

"Oh, no, Gran. Like I told you, I got me a hunnerd other things goin' along with these peaches. But I thank you for sayin' it." And she was gone.

Gran repeated her question. "Does that boy know what you're fixin' to do?"

"No, Gran, 'cept for the books. I had my hands full, just tellin' him I wasn't first in his mind and him thinkin' I was. He said purtineer what you said he'd say. He didn't want to say nothin', but I made 'im. Then he got started talkin', and it was like uncappin' a fizz bottle, the way it all come out.

"Gran, Johnny can't find him no place 'cause he keeps lookin' at hill land

and it ain't hill land he's a'wantin'. He wants a little farm on bottom land so he can grow fancy garden stuff to sell to town folks. It don't seem right, somehow, for a little, bitty farm in the bottoms to cost more'n a big one on the hill top. Dirt's dirt."

"No, child, but they'd be different kinds'a dirt. I can feel what that boy says, me bein' partial to bottom land, myself. I loved that bottom land'a mine, layin' close in by the river. I'd watch that old river go by, times I'd catch me a fish. Maybe a turtle, whatever I had a mind to.

"Yesssiiirrreee, once we got past that first cold winter, that cabin was made good and cozy. Raised me three boys to manhood, right there. Saw me two of 'em take right off and build big houses and raise church-goin' families. Don't know nothin' about t'other one.

"Yessiirree, I loved me that bottom land farm. So that Johnny be wantin' bottom land, huh?"

Amy nodded. "Yeah, Gran, but it'll cost more'n he's got to be spendin'. That'd be a reason why we ain't gettin' married for a long time, and me goin' to work, that'd be a help to get him his land."

"You? How come?"

"Gran, 'member that verse about the special woman lookin' around for the right field and then buyin' it? I got the notion it was her husband wantin' it and her wantin' him to have whatever he wanted that causedit. She had to have cash money if she was to buy, like the book says. I got'a have cash money."

Gran was sober for a minute, thinking. Then a grin tilted the corner of her mouth and she smiled broadly. She looked at Amy, her eyes twinkling with merriment at the picture the girl had painted on her mind. Then she began to chuckle, and then to laugh. Amy giggled and Gran laughed harder. Then she began to cough. Amy dropped her unpeeled peach into the pan and wiped her hands on her apron, watching Gran. Gran kept coughing. Amy jumped up and began to pound on Gran's back. Finally, with a loud wheeze, Gran caught her breath.

Tears streamed down Gran's cheeks, and still she chuckled. Mama came running to the door.

"Gran's fine, Mama. She just got tickled over somethin'."

Essie grinned with relief. "Amy, honey, you got'a quit makin' Gran laugh so hard. Happen sometime she loose her breath and we can't get it pounded back in 'er."

"Now, Essie, I ain't wantin' to be sayin' how you act to your girl, but this here youngen be a pure pleasure to me and if it comes about I was to die, a'laughin', seems it might'n be a bad way to leave this life."

"All right, Gran, but I get scairt when you commence coughin' like that. Amy, hand one of them peach halves over to Gran, to sooth her throat after all that coughin'."

Amy extended the pan to Gran, and the old woman took one of the juicy peach halves.

Essie paused a minute, then disappeared into the house. Gran ate the fruit and cleaned her hands carefully on her apron. Then she chuckled softly. "You think that woman bent on buyin' that land be plannin' on givin' it to her husband, then? I swear if I don't figure you to be 'bout right. I'd say this one thing, they'd be no doubt in my mind it'd pleasure her a mite, just havin' it to give. Givin' is better'n gettin', 'cause the giver, he got more power. He can say if he wants to give or not, and he can say when and how much. But not the getter, he can't do nothin' but take.

"Yessiirree, it's better to be doin' the givin'. Been a lot'a women, though, insistin' on takin' that part for themselves and leave all the gettin' to their husbands, remindin' him all the time how he got to where he is. 'Course there'd be men knowin' what was goin' on, but goin' along with it for the love of the woman."

Amy nodded, and continued. "I said to Johnny, 'We ain't needin' to waste time lookin' at somethin' that ain't what we want. Gran, he's got $300.00 and it sounds like a lot'a money but it ain't all we need. Gonna need a sight more. I figure it'll take him and me both workin' a whole year to get enough."

Gran sorted through the sewing box for just the right color of thread, then handed the girl the thread and needle. "Wisht I could still see to thread that needle, but it seems them needle eyes keeps gettin' littler and littler.

"Now, Amy Catherine, I don't want to waste time talkin' on things you done got planned out, but I've been goin' forward and backward on this one thing. They's just one more little thing I'll say. If you can keep that boy from buyin' his land till spring time, that'd be a good thing."

"How come, Gran? What'd be special 'bout spring time?"

Gran hesitated. "Too many things to be talkin' about. One thing is to see if it drains right, so you'd need to wait for a winter rain. Then you'd know. And grass. Cattle want to get early grass. Them's two things that says to wait till spring time."

Gran nodded in agreement with her own advice. "Springtime, the time of the yellow daisies. That'd be the time."

"Daisies, Gran?"

"For the weddin', honey. Yellow daisies for your weddin'. You'll stand up there in the church and hold them flowers in your hand. I'll be sittin' close so as's to see better. You'll be purtier'n a yellow daisy."

Gran leaned back in her chair and closed her eyes. The girl would have handed the threaded needle to her, but she had dropped off to sleep.

Amy returned to the peach peeling wondering what Gran was trying to say. What did yellow daisies have to do with Johnny's farm? When she finished, she tiptoed away to let Gran sleep. In the kitchen, her mother took the peeled peaches from her.

"Honey, I want you to take that bucket'a peach pits out to the garden and pour 'em along in the furrow of the last row. I drove a stake in the row where I quit plantin' the apple seeds. You start pourin' 'em there and then drag a little dirt over 'em."

Mama smiled brightly, "Happen they'll some of 'em sprout this fall and come spring they'd be up to saplin' size, makin' more trees than you and Johnny'll ever need at your place." Mama's voice trailed off and Amy felt a lump rising in her throat. She turned to face her mother and lowered her head. Mama came to her and circled her daughter's shoulder with her arm, careful not to get peach juice from her hand onto the girl's dress.

"Amy, honey..."

Amy leaned against her mother's shoulder and sobbed. "How come it is, mama? How come I commence to cry when I think on things I want to happen? It don't seem right."

Mama nodded, "But that'd be the way of it. Women cry, from time to time, not knowin' what the cryin' be caused by. Happen some of the time it's 'cause we don't see nothin' ahead we know anything about. Like steppin' into the nighttime dark 'thout a lantern to see to step by. But Amy, darling, cryin' about somethin' we don't know about, it don't stop us none. We just step right on out there in the dark, and if we don't fall, we take another step. That'd be what a woman does."

"But, mama, what happens when we fall?"

"Why, darlin' girl, that'd be when we get right back up! Can't be layin' on the ground and not doin' nothin'. Likely we'd get stepped on, don't you reckon?"

Amy flashed mama a smile and was gone with the buckets. Mama sighed and stared out the window at the blue mountain peaks while peach juice dripped from her hand onto her apron and onto the floor, unnoticed.

Amy carried the two buckets across the yard. She set the seeds by the garden gate and carried the bucket of peach peelings to the hog pen to be poured into the trough amid the squealing, grunting mass of live pork.

She hung the peeling bucket over the gatepost and took the seeds into the garden. She walked past where the plums pits were planted, then the pears, and last, the apples. Mama had a stick standing up in the row and Amy started there, pouring a thick stream of peach seeds in the furrow. With a hoe, she pulled dirt over the seeds and tamped them in by walking down the row three times. Some would sprout in the fall warmth of the garden, others would be cracked by the winter frost and sprout in the spring, allowing them to grow into what would be a fruit orchard for herself and Johnny. She rinsed the buckets at the pump and hung them in the shed.

When she reached the front porch again, Gran's hands were still and her head hung forward, limply. Amy hurried across the porch to lay a hand against Gran's neck at the pulse point. Gran startled awake and picked up the needlework.

"Just dozed off a mite there, child. Seems to be takin' more rest to keep me goin' that it needs to."

Amy suggested, "You could lie down on the bed for a while, Gran, then you'd be feelin' better when you got up."

"No, child, I got me things I got'a finish. You draw up them pictures like you said you'd do, 'cause I want'a be gettin' at 'em."

Amy went into the house for the paper and Gran stared at the mountaintops for a second, then she began to stitch the fabric with colored thread.

7

IT WAS COMING on daylight and Amy's waking thought was, "Somehow, I got'a get this hair on top'a my head."

A smattering of raindrops peppered on the metal roof and streamed down the dark windows. Johnny was right. He had thought it was going to rain, and now, sure enough it was. That meant he'd be here in no time at all.

She slipped into her shoes and dress and went to the kitchen where the rest of the family was. Standing before the washstand mirror, she grabbed a handful of taffy hair. She twisted it tightly and pushed it against her head, winding it around and around. From her mouthful of pins, she selected them one at a time, poking them through the wad of hair into the solid interior. The she put the comb and the rest of the pins on the washstand, and leaning over, she shook her head wildly from side to side.

Her pa came through the door with the milk, but stopped still at the sight of his daughter's shaking head. Mama stopped, poised with one last biscuit, over the baking pan and Gran's wrinkles were stretched wide with mirth.

The knot of hair wobbled and wavered and began to slide. The stubborn ends popped out, flipping three hairpins to the floor.

Gran began to chuckle and then to laugh. Mama sighed and pa remembered the pail of milk in his hand.

Amy recombed her hair, gathered it up again and applied more pins. The hair stayed in place until she leaned her head upsidedown again, shaking it wildly. The bun slid from the top of her head and turned over, spilling pins into the wash pan.

Gran's grin faded down to a smile. "Child, it'd seem to me it's that shakin' of your head like a hound dog fightin' a skunk that's bringin' down your hair. Standin' up still'd likely make that knot stay up there."

"But, Gran, I got'a test it here at home. Happen I get to town and forget and move quick like. Down it'd come right in front'a everyone."

"Well, you got yourself a point. Come kneel down here in the front of me. Likely I'd have some luck with it. Never had no trouble with my own, bein' your age."

The frustrated girl sat on the floor in front of Gran while Gran's gnarled fingers gathered the thick mane of hair together. "Beats me, child, how you got such a sight'a hair. Well, you just watch and we'll be gettin' that hair up there." Gran twisted the mass of hair together and held it against Amy's head, reaching for a hairpin. The bun of hair under her hand began to uncoil faster than a cyclone over the mountaintops, spreading itself evenly over the girl's shoulders.

Gran sighed, "Plain to see, we gonna have to make us two twists."

She divided the hair, twisting half of it tightly in her hand. "Now, child, you hold this here part and I'll twist up t'other side."

Amy reached behind her head and held the end of the coiled hair. Gran twisted the other side and took Amy's twisted strand. She wound the two strands together and coiled them into a wide bun. With a practiced hand, she pushed the coil against her granddaughter's head, tucking the ends under the coil. All around the coil, she secured the mass with closely placed hairpins until it was solid.

"There you be, child. That looks right purty. Happen you'll need a sight more pins than most. That hair of yourn has a mind to be contrary like the mane of a wild horse, and you'd best take along a ribbon 'cause it most likely ain't gonna stay up all day."

Amy looked in the washstand mirror and tilted her head from side to side. "That looks real good, Gran. Only one thing still bothers me."

"What's that, child?"

"If I was to try to do this and you not be here, I'd be needin to have three hands which I ain't got."

"Now, youngen, where at's your figurin' head? You think the Good Lord give you that mouth just for chatterin'? You got'a twist up one part and hold the end'a that in your teeth and then do t'other part. Speck it'll get easier after a time. Never had to do it, myself, not havin' that much hair, but I seen women do it. Mind you don't be shakin' your head or it'll be on your shoulders again."

"Sure, Gran."

Pa's voice came from the front of the house. "Amy, you hear that noise of the dogs a'settin' it up? Johnny's got the lamps on the buggy. Speck that's what set the dogs off."

Amy Catherine gathered the picnic basket over one arm and her handbag in the other hand, walking only slightly slower in deference to the newly let down skirt and the tight cumberbund at her waist. Gran struggled to her feet and hobbled to the front door as the excited girl hugged her mama and scurried across the dewy grass in the early morning light. She set the basket in the buggy, grabbed a handful of skirt out of the way, stepped on a wheel spoke and skid over to the seat of the buggy. She waved to the house and Brushy turned the buggy toward the valley.

"Essie, that child do have a sight of git up and go," Gran observed.

The buggy had disappeared behind the trees but still Amy's mama watched the place where it had been, hesitating to go back inside.

Gran eased out the door and stood beside her. Essie spoke softly, as if to herself. "I sure find myself of two minds about that girl, and it sure don't make me feel easy."

"What two minds you be on, Essie?"

"Gran, that girl got to be sixteen years old and here I stand seein' her ride off in the dark, alone with a young man. Part of me's thinkin' I should'a made out to go along with them two, them not married, and all. The t'other part'a me says what'd be different today from yesterday and the day before, with that boy over here all hours and me not afraid about her bein' safe. What'd you reckon folks'd be sayin' if they was to know I let my onliest little girl be goin' off from mornin' dark to nighttime dark, just her alone with a young man and her sixteen already?"

Gran paused a moment. "Essie, I never wanted to have no say over that girl, you doin' the good job'a raisin' her like you done. But if she was my youngen, I don't reckon I'd be havin' me no thought at all, her bein' what she is. That girl, she's like a race horse, full of plans and dreams, and if she was of a mind that her own mama didn't trust her to be what she ought'a be, that'd weigh on her. She'd likely think her mama to be right, and if mama thought she wasn't to be trusted, then likely she wouldn't be. That'd be a thing you'd not want."

The younger woman nodded, comforted. "Thank you, Gran, for sayin' that to me. It eases my mind so I can go on about my work. It's early yet, so let's sit for a minute on the porch in the cool. I don't seem to have the 'want to' to get started."

Together the two women sat on the swing, staring into the early light. A beam of yellow from the kerosene lamp shone through the window, illuminating their faces. Essie looked at Gran and saw tears streaming down her face.

"Why, Gran, don't you go to cryin' over that youngen. You, yourself, told me she was gonna be safe. You just now said it."

"Essie, honey, it ain't that child causin' me tears. It'd be you and what I done to you, and me just now realizin' it."

"Gran, what you talkin' 'bout? You never done nothin' but good to me and you know it."

"No, Essie, that ain't so. I watched you takin' care'a my baby boy and all them boys of yourn, being busy as a anthill from mornin' till whenever, and me gettin' to have all that time with your own little girl, bein' time that ought'a gone to you. While you was doin' all that work, it was me as got to tramp around in the woods, lookin' for hicker nuts and tellin' her names of the flowers. It was me as got to show her how to make a tight stitch as'd hold up under strain and to show her what kind'a clouds make rain and which ones are just foolin' around. All them years, it was me being' selfish, makin' up for not havin' me a little girl'a my own. All that time, I should'a been takin' the load off you so you could be tellin' her them things. It'd be your right as her mama. I was wrong to do that to you."

Essie listened patiently as Gran poured out her apology. "Now, Gran, I only done work that had to be done by me, and there weren't no way you could'a done my work. You spendin' time with my little Amy Catherine was extra help she got that she wouldn't'a got with you not bein' here. When a woman gets herself a little girl on the tail end'a five boys, she don't hardly know what to do with her and ain't got the time to figure it out. You done helped me with them boys when you give them that weddin' present money to get wagons and mules and things men needs.

"It'd weigh heavy on me, them not havin' things to get a proper start. 'Sides, Amy and me, we had our times now and again, and it was a pleasure to me, goin' about my work, knowin' you was there to look after her and teach her what you know.

"Like this thing about lettin' her go off alone, 'thout me or her pa goin' along, was a bother to me. How's a mama to know from one minute to the next when things is different? Them youngens been together from the time that girl could crawl, and me thinkin' they was safe, when does a mama say, "'Johnny, you been a good boy ever since I knowed you, but now you ain't to be trusted with my girl.' Likely he'd be sayin'. 'Miz Darnell, somethin' be wrong with your girl that she be in danger today when she was not that a'way, yesterday? 'Cause there ain't been no changes in me, and I ain't never hurt her before. Don't reckon this'd be the day I was a'fixin' to start.' And, Gran, he'd be right to say it, and likely his mama'd never be a friend of mine again and I'd have no right to blame her on account of it.

"So when I ask her pa, her own flesh and blood, and he don't know no more'n me, and says to me, 'I don't know about women and never did. If we was talkin' about one of the boys, I'd be sayin' to you not to worry, none. I done talked to them boys and told 'em they'd be treatin' every girl just like she was their sister, till the time they gave 'em a ring on their finger, and if they didn't do that, and if I was to find it out, and I would, they'd not have to worry none about doin' it no more. They'd not be breathin' too good if I was to find it out.' And then he said to me, 'I reckon Johnny's pa done told him the same thing. But I don't know no words to say to a girl, or if maybe we should one of us quit our work and go along.'

"So, you can see that didn't help to set my mind at ease, none. You helped to ease my thinkin', helpin' to put reasons to the words on why I shouldn't have to worry. It'd be like a girl, what ain't been bad, havin' to have a whippin' so as to keep the thought of it out'a her. To my mind, that'd be the way to make her want to see what all that bad was about, her bein' punished for it already.

"Well, Johnny's gone, now, takin' my baby girl and I got me things to get done. Reckon I'll be doin' 'em, now that my mind's clear."

8

OUT ON THE dark, muddy road, Brushy lowered his head into the sudden hard shower of rain and plodded dejectedly on. The oilskin side curtains on the buggy were snapped together, leaving only a space for the reins. A small, semi-transparent isinglass window furnished a forward view of the road and the horse, but Johnny ignored it. Brushy knew his way around. If he was on top of Five-Mile-Hill, he knew he must go down. If he was down, the only way was up. If he was at home, he would be headed for the Darnell's house, and if there, and it was very late at night, surely he would be heading home to the shed and the feedbag. He was now on a road, and he knew to go forward. He shook his head as large drops fell on his forelock and streamed through his eyelashes. The softened red clay of the road sucked at his hoofs. Shaking it away, put him in danger of loosing his footing on the slippery road bed. The wheels of the buggy slid on the clay, falling into, and climbing out of, old ruts.

"Whoa, there!" Johnny called as the downhill slope of the road increased. "Hold back, there! Back! BACK!"

Brushy stiffened his legs, obediently, straining back against the traces, but he was just a pony and the weight of the buggy propelled him onward. The gummy, red clay caked up on the buggy wheels, and turned over and over until giant clods were built up. Then the clods began to break away in large sections by their own weight, creating a feeling inside the buggy of riding on square wheels. The buggy rocked from side to side, shifting its passengers violently about.

Amy put one foot on either side of the wicker picnic basket and held to the handle beside her seat. "Johnny, come dinner time, we gonna need to be six people to eat up all mama put in the basket."

The buggy began to slide precariously forward as Brushy stumbled, causing a lurch as it slipped into a rut. The rear of the buggy began to slide toward the ditch. Johnny grabbed the wheel brake and strained backward, calling, "Easy, boy! Easy, now!'" He watched intently though the tiny window as Bushy's scrambling feet sought a foothold. Regaining his balance, the pony pulled away from the ditch, drawing the buggy back into the road. Johnny eased off the wheel brake.

"I'll be five," Johnny volunteered.

"You'll be what?"

"I'll be five of them people you need to eat our picnic dinner. You can be one. I smell fried chicken."

Amy grinned, "You smell right. Mama cooked us a whole chicken, 'cept for the livers she saved out for Gran. Then we got bread and butter and dill pickles. Got a whole pound cake and four peaches. You think maybe that'd be enough?"

"Maybe. If it ain't, likely we'd be close by some store where we could buy more."

"Aw, Johnny!" Amy playfully punched his shoulder. Johnny reached out to tap her in response, but she ducked way, bumping against the far side of the buggy.

"Aw, pshaw! Now you done it!" she wailed.

"Done what?" Johnny demanded, looking toward her. In the dim light within the closed buggy, he saw her holding her head with both hands. "What's the matter? You hit your head on somethin'?"

"No, I didn't hit my head! It's my hateful, old hair! I feel it a'slidin'. The ends of them pins is stickin' in my head from every which'a'way.

Look at it! Them twists Gran made is unwinding 'like they got a life'a their own!" moaned the girl in dismay.

Johnny tried not to watch. It was shameful, somehow, to watch a woman moaning in agony over her hair. He stared straight ahead and fiddled with the reins, trying not to glance toward Amy. He tried to keep his eyes on his hands, but the fascination was too great.

From the corner of his eye, he saw the coil of taffy hair work itself away from the restraint of the pins and loop down over one eye. A moment later, the other coil followed. Hairpins rained into Amy's lap and onto the buggy seat. Johnny ducked his head and bit his lip.

"Don't you dare do no laughin', Johnny Scott! You just mind your own business," she demanded.

But it was already too late. By now, one coil of hair had unwound and spread itself over her shoulder and the other loop hung down over one ear. Amy's chin was set, firmly and stubbornly. Johnny turned away to study the ditch outside through the tiny window beside his shoulder. His chin began to tremble and his shoulders to shake. A chuckle of mirth formed in his throat and made the corner of his mouth twitch. Having once started, he could not stop. He knew he was on dangerous ground, but that made no difference.

Amy glared fiercely at him, a frown furrowing her forehead. She began to giggle, then to laugh. She laughed until tears flowed down her cheeks. Pulling the ribbon from her pocket, she gathered the hair into a handful at the nape of her neck and tied it securely. Now that the hair was down and her dignity destroyed, there were other options. She kicked off her shoes and drew her feet up under the newly lengthened skirt and leaned comfortably into the corner of the buggy seat.

The rain had slacked off with the coming of daylight. Clouds were melting and in the distance, a beam of sunshine worked through the cloud cover. The stream of sunshine striking the distant mountaintops turned them into diamonds, sparking in the rain-washed air.

"Johnny, look at that sunshine! We gonna have us a good day. Likely, Jacksonville'll be clear'a showers, come time we get there."

"Most likely."

Johnny unsnapped the oilskin side flaps and folded them away. The fresh, wet morning breeze fanned their faces as Brushy trotted long the road at the foot of the hills, following the contours of the river. It was mostly flat land from here to Jacksonville, almost twelve miles away, and they should make very good time.

Johnny broke the silence. "Been doin' me some thinkin'. When we get to Jacksonville, I could check at the courthouse where they post 'for sale' notices just to see what a piece of bottom land'd go for. Wouldn't'a been worth while to make a trip just for that, but bein' we're there anyway, I might just take care of that."

Amy nodded. "I 'speck you could do that. Then we'd have an idea what we're up agin."

Johnny glanced sidelong at her liberal use of "we", but said nothing. It was much too early in the day to risk getting something started that might be tough to handle. Better to just enjoy the day.

The sun was now shining brightly on the buggy and on Brushy's rounded rear. Occasional whiffs of vapor arose from the pony's flanks as the sunshine evaporated the moisture left by the rain.

The river beside the road flowed full and wide, rushing through the narrows and flattening on the plains. Spring rains could send the water gushing and roaring past, clutching at roots of trees and dragging leaves and gravel into its stream. Sycamore trees lined the banks, their cool fragrance strong on the morning air, and willows had crept in thickly wherever a spot of sunshine was to be had.

"You thinkin' to eat something a'fore we get there? Or what?"

"You hungry, Johnny? We got a'plenty for now and later, both. You pick a spot to stop and I'll unpack."

The roadbed had narrowed and now jutted over toward the river to circle around an overhanging bluff. Worn tracks in the grass indicated a favorite stopover spot. Johnny reined Brushy over to a sycamore tree and pulled him to a halt, as Amy, picnic basket over one arm and skirt tail over the other, leaped lightly from the buggy to the deep grass. Johnny wrapped the reins around the tree and followed.

The deep grass was springy beneath their feet. Johnny reached down to pull up a clump of it and to study the dirt clinging to its roots. He sniffed at the dirt, even touching his tongue to it. The pungent acidity of the soil was sharp against his tongue. He crumbled the dirt, letting it fall to the ground from between his fingers.

"Amy, this here'd be the kind of land we need, just like I had wadded up in my hand. There'd be no stoppin' of the garden stuff this here dirt'd grow." He lifted another handful of the black soil. "Here, lean over and smell this."

She obediently sniffed the soil in his hand. The moist smell of the natural organic decay made her sneeze. "That'd be what you want, for sure?"

Johnny nodded. "Wantin' and gettin' be two different things, but if I had me land like this, I'd be hard put to think on somethin' else to want." He looked out over the rolling river for a long moment, then rubbed his eyes and turned to Amy.

"Where at is the fried chicken? I'm emptier'n a rain barrel in August."

Johnny ate the crunchy fried chicken and thick slices of lightbread spread with butter. He looked down and dug his toe into the soft dirt. That Amy and her talk! Before she made him talk about what he wanted, they would have been chatting about this and that, and he would have been reasonably content. But look at him now! Sitting here, silently studying the dirt under his feet. This lovely, deep soil just laying there, doing no one any good.

Amy nibbled a chicken wing and studied Johnny's face. She realized with crystal clarity that she truly was not first with Johnny and she would never be first, until he got his land. How wise Gran was! She clinched her teeth and squared her dimpled chin. When a woman knew for sure what she had to do, it made the doing of it a lot easier. Now Amy knew. For sure!

It was late morning when they neared Jacksonville. The gravel road gave way to a street of herringbone brick. Brushy's dainty hoofs clopped and clicked to the grind of the buggy wheels. Tall brick buildings with plate glass fronts lined Main Street. The store windows were decorated with dresses and stoves, hats and harnesses, toys and wash boilers. Everything in the world was right before their eyes and could be bought, if a body only had enough money.

Brushy was tied with many other horses, some saddled and others hitched to wagons, in a tree-shaded lot at the edge of town. His passengers left him and went to explore the wonders of the city. They walked down one side of Main Street and back up the other, gazing in amazement at the displays in the store windows.

Johnny pointed, "See, there's the big sign showin' that ice cream cone. We gonna get us one of them 'afore we leave to go home."

"What flavor you gonna get?"

"Don't know yet. Maybe three different, like the picture."

"There it is, over there!"

"There is what?"

"That's the book store. See that sign? Hurry!"

Johnny was forced to step up his pace to keep up with her as she cut across the street without going to the corner. He tried to get her attention, "I say, Amy. Likely we was supposed to be down at the corner 'afore we crossed." But his words were lost, because she was across the street before he finished what he was saying, so it really didn't matter, anyway.

The bookstore smelled dusty and new, of wool carpets and printer's ink. There were rows and rows of books with shiny new covers setting on shelves that reached from the floor to the ceiling. Amy could only stand and stare in amazement, speechless for once.

"May I help you?" a man's voice asked.

The dazed girl could only mutter, "Oh, I don't know."

"She wants to buy a book," Johnny came to the rescue.

The man smiled at Johnny, "Any particular book?"

Johnny shrugged and looked at Amy. The man looked from one to the other and waited.

Amy found her voice. "I got the names wrote down." She drew a piece of worn paper from her pocket. "I want Advanced Spelling, Principles of Mathematics, English Composition, Adventures in Literature and Complete World History."

Johnny stared at her, open mouthed and pale, but the clerk nodded, knowingly. "You need the school books for the eighth grade, I see."

"Yes, sir, but I need the books for the seventh grade, too."

"But they're not on your list. That would be another five books."

Amy thought for a minute. "But I only went to the sixth grade. My teacher wrote down these books he said I'd be needin'."

"Could your teacher have been Mr. Campbell from River Bend School? I know him well."

Amy brightened, "That's him."

"Then I suspect you are getting ready for the teacher's certification. Mr. Campbell apparently thinks you're quick enough at your studies to skip the seventh grade books."

Amy stared in indecision at the books lining the shelves. What should she do now? She had counted on the old teacher to tell her everything she needed. What now?

Johnny had sat down on one of the chairs near the window. He was still somewhat pale as he watched the clerk gather the books from their various places on the shelves. He watched as the clerk piled them on the counter making a stack he judged to be close to a foot high. There was sure to be years of struggle, just to read all of them and surely his good times with his girlfriend were a thing of the past.

Amy ignored the books she was going to buy and began to pull volume after volume from the shelves, examining each with interest before returning it. One large book showed a pair of hands on the cover. Each picture inside showed the hands in various positions.

"Look, Johnny. This book is all about hands."

Johnny looked, uncomprehendingly.

The clerk now had all the books together and was watching Amy. "That book is for teaching a special language to children who can't hear. Each of those signs stands for a word or group of words. That's the way deaf children learn their lessons from a teacher who knows the signs. They can learn to talk with each other and with anyone who knows the sign language."

"Oh. I never did hear about that. I guess I just never knowed persons who couldn't hear."

The clerk wrote down the price of each of the five books. "That'll be $12.80." He looked first at Amy, then at Johnny. Then Amy looked at Johnny.

Johnny stood up weakly and removed his money clip from his pocket. He peeled off two five dollar bills and three ones, holding out his hand for the change.

Amy proudly picked up the books. "Thank you, mister."

Johnny followed her from the bookstore, saying nothing.

Amy asked, "You thinkin'a goin' over to that ice cream store right now?"

Johnny considered it but hesitated. "Uh, I'd sooner wait a spell till my stomach settles down a mite. Reckon it'd be more enjoyable if we'd wait a bit."

"You feelin' sick, Johnny? That bookstore make you sick? The way it smelled funny, the wool carpet and all?"

"Weren't the store, itself, actually. Just glad to be back outside again."

"Then what you think we ought'a do, now?"

"See that court house square? They got the posted notices in there for land that's for sale. Wanted to see them, like we talked about. You want me to tote them heavy books for you?"

Amy hugged the books to her chest. "Oh, no, carryin' these here books'd be no trouble to me a'tall. A sick man like you might just drop 'em right in the middle of the street."

"Well, we could take 'em over and leave 'em in the buggy."

Amy shook her head. "Told you these books weren't no trouble to me."

The bulletin board was covered with notices. Everything from land to animals to farm equipment was posted there. There were farms and unimproved tracts of land. There was hill land, bench land, riverside tracts and large and small acreages. Some had cabins and water wells on them.

"This'n here, it'd be up by the Bend. Twenty-five acres on a slope and it'd sell for $35.00 an acre. That'd be $875.00 all told."

"Whew!"

"Here's another'n."

"That'n says $30.00 an acre and it don't say it has no spring."

"Lookie at this'n, Amy. Got 40 acres and it's $5.00 an acre. What's that figure to? See, there's a cabin and two everlastin' springs. That'd save a heap'a time with no cabin to put up 'afore the spring crops go in."

Amy looked at Johnny as she shifted the weight of the books from one hip to the other. "Johnny, listen to me. You been trampin' over every hill in this countryside, lookin' at farms. Not one of them pieces of land you looked at up there took your eye so what'd make you think this'n be any different? If you really wanted what you just described to me, you'd have it done an' bought and you and me'd be livin' there, not standin' here talkin'. You got that much money in your pocket right now. You just go on and buy it but don't be blamin' me for not havin' the feelin' you get when you dig your shoetoe into that black, riverside land. You hear me?"

Johnny ignored her and continued to look at the notices. "Look at this'n. Appears to be a honey of a place, but they're askin $50.00 an acre."

"Likely worth it, too."

Johnny continued to read. "Got twelve acres to it. What'd that be, total?"

Amy waited as Johnny frowned and worked out the sum in his head. "That'd be $600.00, and I'd have to put a cabin. If I worked at wages for a year and put it with what I have, we could look at somethin' like that. 'Course, good land like that'd be snapped up 'afore the year was up."

The girl nodded. "Likely right on that. And most likely there'd be another one as good or better, stuck up there in the place of it come time we have that much money."

Johnny sighed and ran his calloused fingers through his dark hair as he turned back to the bulletin board. "Lookie at this notice. Matched Clydesdales. You got a scrap'a paper so I could put down how to find these horses?"

Amy dug into her pocket and came up with the worn paper containing the list of books. "Take this. Won't need to be rememberin' the names of these books no more." She heaved the weight of the precious cargo to the original hip.

Johnny began to copy the map the owner of the Clydesdales had drawn to help locate them. "Wisht I knowed the cost of them horses."

"You think you'd be needin' a pair of big horses like them Clydesdales? What kind'a crop you fixin' to put in? Likely they go for a lot'a money, or they'd be already sold to a neighbor. If they still got 'em, and if they needed to bring a notice over here, likely they'd be more money than most folks be wantin' to pay."

"Most likely. Gonna look at 'em, anyway. Always wanted to see me one of them horses, close up like." Johnny crammed the map into his pocket and kept looking.

Amy tried to be patient. "Sight of the things folks are wantin' to sell," she commented. "This'n's a baby cradle, and that'n has a machine that does the washin' all by itself. That's what it says. Sight of what a body can see and want for, just standin' here readin' notices."

Johnny nodded. "I'm gettin' empty in the middle. You ready to eat that ice cream cone?"

"Been ready for an hour. Just been standin' here waitin' on you to feel better and get used to not havin' that money you paid for these books." Amy teased, unmercifully.

"Now, Amy, you stop that! I said I'd be payin' for them books, and I did."

"Yep, and you was turnin' green enough to be sick, right there on the floor of the store."

"Hush, and come on. I reckon I better hold onto you while we cross this street, so you don't run out there and get them books all ruined."

"Well, Johnny Scott, we ought'a be about even, tit for tat. Don't you be tryin' to get any more word licks in on me, 'cause my tongue, bein' faster, I can best you at that game, every time." She grinned at Johnny, but extended her free hand which Johnny carefully ignored as they crossed the street together.

They stood side by side before the counter, studying the flavors. "Chocolate, vanilla and strawberry. That one says honeydew and there's peppermint. Hmmmm."

The clerk waited, patiently.

Johnny placed the order. "We want us two cones like that one in the picture with chocolate and vanilla on the bottom and strawberry on top."

"Both of 'em just alike?"

"Yep."

With cones in hand, they left the ice cream store and crossed again to the courthouse square. They sat on the wooden benches in the shade of tall trees while the cool murmur of the fountain, splashing in the goldfish pond, blended with the calls of the crickets in the trees. The clop of horse hoofs on the brick streets added to the excitement and festivity of the day.

"Hmmmm, always did love store bought ice cream better'n anything." Johnny managed the cone with his left hand and raised his right arm to the back of the bench behind Amy. The girl squirmed a mere two inches away from him.

"Johnny Scott, you aimin' to get me talked about? You be wantin' to marry a girl you made a scandal of? A body'd think you had enough to do, eatin' that ice cream cone." The dimple in her chin deepened as a smile softened the rebuke.

"Eatin' ice cream ain't no trouble to me."

"Reckon not, the way you're puttin' it down."

Thus dismissing the subject of conduct, Amy settled down to the enjoyment of the ice cream. She nibbled the edge of the crunchy cone. "Beats me how a body could make somethin' so light and crackly and still strong enough to hold up the ice cream. Look at them little flakes and how there's air down there. Ain't even solid."

"Yep."

Amy's tongue sampled all three flavors. "Swear, I don't know which flavor I like best."

"No need to choose."

"Reckon not."

"You know, I ain't for sure one of them cones is gonna be enough to fill up my holler spot."

"You thinkin' on gettin' another one?"

"Yep. Thought I'd try me that peppermint. Never had nothin' but candy that was flavored with peppermint."

Amy nodded. "Wisht I could take one to Gran, that bein' her favorite flavor. Reckon it'd be long melted, time we got it home."

"Reckon so. You gonna want another one?"

"Wisht I could but this'n gonna 'bout fill me up."

Johnny hesitated, watching her eat.

Amy reconsidered, "But if you was to get another'n, you could put one dip of honey dew in top of yourn and I'd take it."

"Sure, that'd do it. You sit here with them books and I'll be back."

The girl leisurely licked the dip of chocolate ice cream in pleasurable meditation. The bench was comfortable, the shade was deep and cool and the sights around her were as satisfying to her eyes as the ice cream was to her tongue. Her left hand absently caressed the hard, cloth-bound covers of the books stacked beside her. She had the feeling that this was the pleasant rest period she was permitted before beginning the long climb upward. It would be hard work, studying alone, but she would do it. She would do whatever else needed doing, just like her mama and Gran had done. Of course, it would be a while before her biscuits tasted like her mama's. So lost in thought she was, that she was somewhat startled back to reality as Johnny sat down heavily beside her.

There, balanced on top of his cone, was the ball of golden ice cream called honeydew. She reached her well, nibbled cone toward his and nudged the ball of ice cream from his cone onto hers. She stroked it lightly with her tongue. "Hmmm, never tasted nothin' like this one. Puts me in the mind of muskmelon, or maybe pumpkin pie without much spice." She extended the cone toward Johnny, "There, taste it right there."

Johnny licked the ice cream. "Beats me if you ain't right. Tastes like pumpkin custard with top milk, or maybe a muskmelon been soakin' in the spring."

They finished the ice cream and sat silently on the bench for a few minutes.

"Been thinkin' it'd be 'bout time to get a little water for Brushy. He's likely gettin' lonesome and dry."

"Think we ought'a be goin' on home?" Amy suggested, with some reluctance. "We got a long way ahead of us."

Johnny sighed, "Speck so. Don't seem like I'm in no hurry, though. Have to stop somewhere along the way and finish up that chicken and cake."

"Yeah, but I don't see that as any big chore. Don't see you havin' no trouble on that score."

They walked along the brick sidewalk surrounding the courthouse square and crossed the street into the shaded field. Brushy saw them in the distance, and whinnied in greeting. The sound brought on a vocal symphony as the other bored horses and mules shook their harnesses and looked for their own drivers. They snorted and stomped, finally settling down to wait a bit longer. Brushy tossed his head in anticipation.

"Old Brushy, boy, you gettin' dry? You glad to see us a'comin'?" Johnny's hand stroked Brushy's muzzle. Amy climbed into the buggy and Johnny led the pony to the hollow log watering tough.

At the trough, Brushy blew a huff of breath to scatter the gliding spiders from the surface of the water and drank in long, grateful gulps.

He raised his head high, allowing the water from his mouth to drizzle down his neck, then lowered his head to the water, again.

"Amy, just had me a thought. Would you bring down that canteen bottle and we'll fresh it up from this pump. Likely, that water we brung is warm as bath water in that bottle."

Refreshed and back on the brick streets, Brushy lifted his hoofs high as he proudly bore his passengers along. Johnny permitted the pony the opportunity to show off, arching his neck and lifting his tail slightly, permitting the glossy brown brush of it to glide from side to side. His dark plume of mane rippled and flowed with the movement of his proud head. The sound of his hoofs was a rhythmic clickity-click above the grind of the wheels.

Heads turned and watched as the little paint pony and the neat, well-kept buggy drew the young couple through the streets. Some looked forward to the day when they would have a rig so fine, others recalled similar rigs from a rosy memory, protected by years of time. Others just watched and sighed as a pleasant scene passed before their eyes

Bricks gave way to gravel as the road turned east toward the town of River Bend, and Brushy lowered his tail and straightened his neck, preparing for the long haul. The small hoofs slowed to a steady clop, clop, better suited to the trek home.

The sun was still high and shone through the back window of the buggy. It glared off the multiple shades of green in the grass and trees on either side of the road. The blues of the sky and distant mountaintops blended their hues with the blue of the river beside them. The brown road pulled them forward. It would be twelve miles of flat land to get to River Bend, then five miles uphill to their mountaintop homes.

They rode in silence, relaxing from the excitement of the day. When they were two miles from River Bend, Johnny suggested, "This'd be a good stoppin' place. Need to let Brushy rest and graze a little, 'afore we take on that hill."

"Wait, Johnny. Go on around that clump of outcrop rocks. That's where Gran and Grandad had their land… the place Gran sold off when Grandad died. Pa grew up on that land and said things about how happy Gran was, livin' there. She'd be like you, thinkin' bottom land was better than land in the hills. She tells stories about that land bringin' her pleasure just watchin' it, happen she had a minute to spare. 'Course, raisin' three boys, she likely didn't have too many spare minutes."

The buggy crunched along, circling the jutting bluff where they had eaten on the way in to town. The road leveled and straightened, following the low hills. They rode along on the road, just a few hundred feet from the river.

Amy slipped her feet from her shoes and drew them up under her, as her eyes searched for a familiar landmark.

"There!" she said, suddenly. "I 'member that clump'a cedars. There's flat land twixt the road and the river, good for a picnic for us and Brushy, too."

They circled the curve and Johnny drew Brushy to the side of the road. The rushing river rolled and foamed, surging against the grassy bank not more than 300 feet from the road. The force of the water struck at the roots of a stand of willow trees before straightening and heading on down toward River Bend. Opposite the river, the land climbed in a gradual flatish slope toward the hills. Trees of pine and cedar clustered at the base of the hills, guarding a comfortable looking house and a large barn. Smoke arose from the chimney of the summer kitchen built away in the back, so summer canning would not heat the house unbearably. Black and white cows munched contentedly along the fence line.

Johnny gazed in admiration. "That'd be one purty lay'a land. Ain't no wonder Gran liked livin' here. Be a mite'a work to take care of, but them with three boys, that'd be help. Where at was her home place?"

The girl frowned in concentration. "Gran and Grandad had a cabin in a grove'a cedars. She liked the way them trees smelled after a shower. Had a big cabin. Saw it one time when I was little and Pa brought me and the boys down here to see it. It was up the edge of the hill, somewhere. I was little and don't rightly remember."

Johnny rubbed his chin, thoughtfully. "I'd'a thought your Pa'd'a wanted this piece of land, come time his pa passed on."

Amy shrugged. "Reckon not. Time Grandad passed on, he already had him a good place and him and the boys had crops in the field, so they must'a thought it better to sell Gran's place and move her up there."

Johnny nodded. "Folks got'a figure the best thing that suits everybody. Be no way to act, just doin' what suited you with no thought to the rest'a the family."

Brushy was left to drag his reins and graze on the deep clover. Johnny wiped his fingers on the tea towel from the basket and helped himself to a chicken leg and a slab of the golden pound cake. He strolled across the deep grass toward the roaring of the river.

The stream was wide at this point. A new concrete abutment had been built on the other side of the river, slightly up stream, in preparation for the building of a trestle bridge across it. The bridge would accommodate the coming Mississippi Central Railway. The river, which had flowed straight and smooth between its banks for centuries, now struck the concrete base of the coming bridge and deflected sharply toward the bank where Johnny stood. The surface of the water had a herringbone appearance as ripples of one direction overlaid those of another current. Johnny bit his lip and studied the pattern of the river surface, dimpling and curling, as deep water followed the channel while surface water coursed toward the bank.

He pulled his eyes away from the fascination of the water to the grass beneath his feet. Amy stood beside him, ignoring the chicken wing in her hand, watching and listening.. "Be a lot'a good grazin' land here, twixt the road and the river. Seems like it could be fenced in and put to use. Could pasture 'im some horses there, if he had a mind to."

Amy suggested, "Reckon this man got 'im enough good land that he don't be needin' this part."

Johnny looked from the swirling river to the grass, almost knee deep and sighed softly as he chewed the last bite of the pound cake. "Saw a spring back there by the road. Gonna get me a drink."

9

HIGH UP IN the mountains, Gran sat on the porch, watching the yellow butterflies check for nectar in the late summer marigolds. The last golden rays of the sun glanced off their wings in golden lights. Looking back to her lap, the old woman picked up the needlework. The bright threads formed the outlines to her granddaughter's drawing as her fingers moved rapidly with the needle. Gran rubbed her faded eyes to rest them. "I been meanin' to thank You, Lord, for all them things You let me do.

"Here I was, thinkin' it'd be quilts, tea towels and pretty underthings I'd need to be makin' for Essie's little girl, but You knowed all along it weren't gonna be that'a'way. Why, I was thinkin' that little girl gonna be a farm jenny, like me. Not complainin', Lord, 'cause I had me a good life, but that girl'a ours, she be a racehorse, pure and simple. She be a'prancin' and a'dancin' right now, not knowin' her own speed. She gonna take off a'runnin' one day and we gonna see nothin'a her but heels and dust." She nodded slowly.

"Lord, I see You had Your hand in what I was a'thinkin' to do with my little piece'a river land.

"I want to be thankin' You, now, for showin' me Your plan, 'afore takin' me on home. That Johnny of her'n, hankerin' after rich, bottom land and him bein' just the fellow for my little girl… Lord, I got'a say, its a sight how well You plan things.

"Now I got'a be gettin' back to work, Lord, if I aim to get this here quilt done. Don't You feel bad, though, 'cause there'll be lots'a talkin' time for You and me, once I get up there with You."

Gran pulled the thread taut and smooth, giving a satiny glow to the needlework in her hand. "Right purty the way that child can draw them pictures," Gran commented to herself, smoothing the block on which two golden butterflies rode the breeze over an orange flower. "Lord, You 'member the look that girl gave me when I said for her to make me yellow butterflies, that bein' what she put me in the mind of, playin' in the yard when she was a mite of a girl?"

Though having been dismissed earlier, God still seemed close to Gran as she continued to talk to Him, friend to friend.

"See there, Lord, how that girl made them pictures? There's that ruby stone to be stitched up in red. That'd not be worth the price of that special woman she's gonna be, like the wise king said. And there's that candle, sayin' sometimes she got'a work when it ain't light. Here's that hand, sayin' she gonna help where she's needed. Traced her own hand she did. See that table, meanin' she'd give food to the hungry? Look at this'n, Lord. That picket fence with the gate, means everyone goin' in or out gonna know about her and how special she is. Gonna take note'a Johnny, too, on account'a her."

Gran sighed with pleasure and piled the new quilt blocks in a neat stack. "Just gonna ask one more thing, Lord. If You'd see it in Your heart to wait till I get this here done a'fore You take me, then we'd have time to say all that needs sayin'."

She reached for the thread basket, selected another color, and painstakingly threaded it into the eye of the needle, squinting her tired eyes in concentration.

10

AT THE FOOT of the mountain, Brushy wandered along, cropping the grass as Johnny finished the last of the food. The little pony was still chewing a mouth full of clover as he pulled the buggy back onto the road and headed toward River Bend.

Johnny frowned and looked toward the house on the slope. "Keep thinkin' I could mention to them folks how the river got to eatin' away at the land back there. Bein' it was mine, I'd want to know so's to do something'."

His passenger responded. "Reckon he wouldn't know already, hearin' the roar that water makes, whippin' and rippin' around like that?"

Johnny didn't answer. He let Brushy set his own pace and glanced sidelong at Amy. Her starched dress was somewhat wrinkled from the activity of the day. She sat on one foot and lounged against the back of the buggy seat, thumbing through one of the new books. A faint smile played at the corner of her mouth as she read a bit here and another passage there.

Johnny nodded slightly, as he told himself, "No need to get in a hurry tryin' to please a girl. Wait, and let her tell you what she wants. Who'd think it would be a book and not a box of chocolates that would put that look on her face. As his thoughts mulled over the mysteries of womanhood, it seemed that it would be better most times to see what she wanted than to surprise her, like other fellows seemed to think their girls liked. The money he spent today would have brought Sunday dresses to last a year but something told him he was points ahead by getting the books.

Finally, Johnny could keep still no longer. "I sure do like ridin' along with you like this, Amy. Wisht you'd take off that ribbon and let your hair hang around your face."

She grinned at him and closed her book. She yanked the end of the ribbon and set loose the bundle of hair that promptly spread over her shoulders.

"Oh, Johnny, you're just sayin' that 'cause I ain't no good at makin' it stay up."

"Nope. I ain't never lied to you and I ain't gonna start now."

The setting sun made a shadow of the buggy that reached up to the rump of the pony. At the foot of Five-Mile-Mill, the little animal turned, without guidance, toward the mountain. Johnny watched Amy and told himself he was the luckiest fellow in the world. They were five miles from home.

"Johnny, I sure want to thank you for gettin' me these books. I'm gettin' skittish to start in on 'em."

Johnny answered, "No thanks needed. I'm mostly glad it ain't me havin' to get the learnin' out of 'em."

Amy sighed, apprehensively. "Likely gonna wish it weren't me, neither, 'afore I get through. Don't know no other way to get me that certificate."

"How long you figure it to take?"

"Wisht I had the answer to that. It'd help me makin' other plans."

"Two years, you think?"

"Maybe, maybe not. Hope not. Got other things to do."

"Amy, I sure like the way you look, sittin' over there. You was even a purty girl when you was little and skinny."

There were four miles to go. The girl leaned against the far side of the buggy.

Johnny continued, "They was times I 'member, I wisht you was my little sister, 'stead'a Dave's. Then, after that, when we got bigger, I was more'n glad you wasn't."

Amy picked up her speller. "I figure to have the most trouble with the speller, and the one on English Composition."

A red squirrel rippled and flowed across the road in front of them. Brushy plodded on.

Johnny commented, "I still got me that paper tellin' where the man with the Clydesdales lives. Wisht I knowed how much they was."

"Likely find out, quick as you go over there."

"Who said I was gonna waste time goin' over there?"

"I figure you to be goin' over there the first afternoon you ain't needed in the field. Seems you'd be a fool not to, seein' as how you're so curious."

"Think so?" Johnny had now learned what he needed to know. Now, he knew she at least approved of the idea of the horses.

"Think you'd want to go along with me?"

"See no reason not to. You studyin' wouldn't keep me from watchin' how purty you look." Johnny touched her ear with his finger.

They were two miles from home.

"Happen mama couldn't let me go, cannin' season bein' here."

"But you'd need to see them horses."

Amy put down the book and faced him. "Johnny, what'd you want them horses for? What you got to do that mules'd be too little to get done?"

"Been thinkin'. When I get it thought out, I can say more." Johnny gave an answer and still bought time. He was proud of himself.

Brushy angled to the edge of the road and mouthed a clump of dusty grass from the roadside. Johnny reined him back to the smoother, middle of the road.

"Amy, how long after Christmas you thinkin' to wait 'afore we can get married?"

One more mile to go. Dusk had settled in and the tree canopy on either side of the road was dark.

"Swear, Johnny, wisht I knowed that, myself. I got thinkin' to do and there ain't no way to know how long it'll take."

Johnny sighed. "Somewhere in all that thinkin', you gonna be decidin' if it's me or someone else you want?"

Amy whirled and turned toward him, drawing both feet under her. Her sudden movement jerked the light buggy, and Brushy turned his head to see the source of the activity.

"Johnny Scott, you think, long as you been knowin' me, that I'd say one thing and do the other? I done said you was the one I wanted. Come time that ain't true, you'd be first to hear it from me." She lifted her chin and looked down her nose at Johnny, the dimple carved deeply into her chin.

"Now, Amy, don't go gettin' huffy. Didn't mean nothin' by what I said."

"Good thing you didn't," she retorted. "The thinkin' I got'a do is concernin' me and no one else. Can't nobody help me figure me out but me."

On that, Johnny was inclined to agree.

They were a quarter of a mile from home. Amy picked up Johnny's hand and held it in her lap. She turned and leaned back, letting her feet drop to the floorboard.

Johnny sat still and breathed deeply. He'd like more clarification on the thinking she planned to do, but decided not to risk asking. Her driveway was just ahead and Brushy began to step faster. Johnny reined him back to a slower pace. She still held his hand. So far, so good.

Brushy turned, without direction, into the lane. Johnny pulled Amy gently toward him. She leaned against his shoulder and put her hand on his cheek.

Brushy stopped at the gate.

"Good night, Johnny," she whispered, letting him kiss her cheek. She turned and gathered her books on one arm and her skirt tail on the other, leaping nimbly to the ground. He noted she had no other hand for the picnic basket, but, no matter, he'd bring it back tomorrow.

Johnny smiled and turned the buggy around. All in all, the day was clearly worth the $12.95 he had spent. If she liked the books, then that was just a plus.

Amy closed the door behind her, suddenly realizing she had forgotten the basket. Oh, well, she'd get it next time.

11

THE SUNSHINE SHONE through the stable door on Brushy's flanks as his tongue scooped up the last grains of corn from the edges of his feed box. Being fed corn in the morning of a summer day meant something was up.

At the end of the driveway, with Johnny on his back, he made a move to turn toward Amy's house, but Johnny reined him toward town, five miles down the hill.

This was a puzzling time in Johnny's life. If he were a man who had just bought a farm, he would be busy doing fall things, getting ready for winter. But here he was, a man still on his pa's place, facing the need to get on with his life and plans.

Brushy trotted and galloped down the hill and clip-clopped proudly along the brick street, arching his neck and swinging his tail. At Johnny's direction, he turned in at a local business bearing the sign, "RIVER BEND COAL COMPANY. We Chute it to You."

Brushy was tied to the hitching rail in front of the building where he waited, switching flies, while Johnny spent along time inside the building.

12

BACK ON THE mountain, Amy's open speller book lay propped beside her on the old porch swing. It would be easier to study if Gran would quit talking.

"Come time we get them pieces all set together and rolled on the frame, I'll not be needin' no more help," Gran promised.

Then she added, "Got me four more pictures in my mind, ready to be done. Look at that spinnin' wheel! Lookin' good. Showin' how the special woman got'a be busy with her hands. That there heart shows how her children and her man gonna love her. Had me some trouble with that'n."

Amy looked up. Sewing the blocks, looking at the speller and listening to Gran was more than she could manage. The spelling would have to wait.

"Now, child, don't you let my ramblin' be disturbin' you none. Lookie here at that picture of a mouth. I like that one, meanin' only kind things is bein' said and there's that purty crown, meanin' she gonna be honored for the things she gonna do."

The girl looked, but noticed something entirely different. "Gran, look at what you done. You finished that middle block and set it in amongst the others. You said it'd have to have the ring on it."

"Now child," Gran assured her, "don't you be frettin'. Time enough for that. This a'way we can see how purty it'll be and not have to wait till we see the actual ring."

"You gettin' anxious to be done, Gran?"

"Feared so, youngen. Always did get anxious to see a new-pieced quilt ready for the stitching. I like this quilt better'n any I ever done, and I done a fair sight of 'em. Special about this'n, is the purty pictures you done. Never had no one with a hand to draw pictures up to now."

Amy's attention wandered. "Gran, Johnny's talkin' like it'd take a year'a work to get money for his land."

"That long? Would'a thought bottom land to not be that much money. Just dirt, like everywheres else."

"Yeah, dirt's dirt, ain't it? Gran, you ought'a see the sight'a things to buy we saw over in Jacksonville. Half them things I wouldn't know how to make use of, happen I had the money to buy 'em."

"Reckon, so, child. All I ever knowed was to make use of what was in my hand and pray the Good Lord I had what I needed most when I needed it."

Amy sewed most of the morning. The blocks forming the top of the quilt were just about set together, and Gran worked, seemingly tireless, on the remaining few to be embroidered.

It was mid-afternoon when Johnny came galloping into the yard on Brushy. It was so unusual to see him come riding so early in the afternoon on a work day, that Amy ran out to meet him.

Over the gatepost, he told her, "I been over to see them Clydesdales, and if there was ever a purty piece of horse flesh, they'd be it. Man owns 'em laughed when I say to him, 'Wait, I want my future wife to see these here horses 'afore I decide if I want to buy 'em.' But they's more to the story than that, and if you can go with me, I'll take Brushy home and get the buggy."

The puzzled girl sensed the importance of the occasion. "Sure enough, Johnny. Hurry back and I'll be ready." She ran back to the house and Johnny galloped away.

By now, the excitement had drawn mama to the porch. "Amy, honey, Miz Scott sick or somethin', the way Johnny went gallopin' off like that?"

"No, mama. Ain't nothin' bad wrong. Johnny just seen a pair'a horses he thinks he might like. Come to get me to look at 'em with him. He's gonna be back with the buggy."

Gran and mama looked at each other, their glances long and puzzled. It was hard to tell which was the stranger action, a grown man off looking at horses in the middle of a summer day, or a man coming to get his girl friend's opinion on the purchase of horses. Amy had dashed off to put on a fresh dress. Essie shook her head and observed, "That Johnny, he's a strange one."

Gran agreed and added. "Likely so, but if that boy thinks he got'a talk with her when he buys a horse, it'd be a sure bet he gonna talk with her on other things when he needs to. A problem most men folks got is not sayin' what they need to be sayin' to their women."

Amy heard none of their comments. She was hurriedly dragging a comb through her hair and wiping a shine on her patent leather shoes.

In hardly a half an hour, Johnny was back. He had left Brushy at home to rest and the buggy was being pulled by a large, rangy mule named Jasper. He looked ridiculously large to be pulling the light buggy, and it was evident that pulling the buggy was not his favorite thing to do.

"Get on out!" urged Johnny to the mule. "Get movin' along, there."

Amy was waiting at the gate and jumped in before the buggy had hardly come to a halt. Then they were on their way, Johnny shouting at Jasper to get a move on.

Gran watched her grandaughter leave and prayed, "Lord, You see that girl? Sure hope You can get a'holt on to her 'afore she gets goin' in the wrong direction. Fast as she moves, she'd likely be past catchin' up with 'afore You can get to her."

Jasper had now caught up to the excitement of the day and danced and sidled all over the road. Jerking his head to one side, he caught the bit in his teeth, making it almost impossible for Johnny to guide him. He raced down the road, the buggy swinging from side to side.

Johnny sighed. "I sure do hate to drive Jasper when he's rested and wound up. No way to get his attention 'thout beatin' the soup out'a him, till he remembers where he gets his orders."

With that, Johnny pulled down the whip from its pocket in the top of the buggy. With a flick of the wrist, he wound the whip full of ripples, bringing them down onto Jasper's gray back. The mule slewed sideways, dropping the bit from his teeth and flinging his head high in an angry whinney.

"You asked for it," Johnny told him and tapped him once more against the flanks. "I ain't in no mood to be foolin' with you. Got other things on my mind."

Jasper lowered his head and curled his lip away from his teeth. He stopped still in the road and shook, jingling the harness and rattling the buggy.

Johnny wound up the whip again, causing it to whistle and sing in the air. Jasper, having no trouble with his ears, thought it was likely time to trot on down the road.

Johnny returned the whip to its pocket.

"Amy, you just got'a have a see at them horses, but that ain't all. Since you promised we gonna be married, figured you'd need to have your say on some other things."

Amy was silent, looking apprehensively at Johnny. He didn't notice.

"I took Bushy down to River Bend, earlier today, lookin' to see a man about I job I heard of. Sure enough, they needed a man with good horses, able to haul loaded wagons out'a the mountains. I told I was their man 'cause I could do just that. Then they tell me that ain't all there is to the job, else they'd'a had a man for it, a long time ago.

"They say to me the man takes this job got'a have strong horses that can hold back, and a dump wagon with a lift tongue.

"I was makin' to leave and they told me they had the dump wagon they'd sell but wasn't gonna be responsible for the horses. A man'd have to have his own. Didn't want no mules, bein' too slow, they said."

Amy couldn't resist a comment. "Should'a showed 'em Jasper after he had 'im a couple days rest."

Johnny grinned, but would not be sidetracked. "I told 'em, could they wait one more day, bein' they waited so long already, and I'd try to get me them horses. They tell me they ain't in that much of a hurry, the job not startin' for another month."

Johnny drew a deep breath and paused, unaccustomed to such long speeches with such important consequence attached. "So I say to 'em, 'Just what's to be hauled in that wagon?' and they tell me its just coal, but they say the man got'a take the wagon up the hill and bring down coal in chunks.

"That's when I say to 'em I ain't no miner, but they say all I got'a do is pick it up and put it in the wagon. They got other men to muck it out'a the mountain. Then the wagon got'a be brought back down the mountain careful. Light horses'd not be enough to hold back on the weight'a the load. Need big horses. They say do I want the job.

"I say maybe if there was money enough in it.

"They say three dollars for every day at the start and more later if they don't have no trouble out'a me. Told 'em to get ready with more money 'cause I ain't never been no trouble to nobody since I was a little fellow, worryin' my mama."

Johnny let Amy digest the information. She waited.

"Amy, would ya pick up that paper down at your feet and lookie at them figures. I put 'em down quick, bein' on the move, but I think they're right. Three dollars a day for six days makes $18.00 every week.

"Them Clydesdales I looked at, sell for $75.00 each, makin' $150.00 and the wagon gonna sell for $17.00. I got up to $167.00, so far. It'd be way up in the fall 'afore I earned that much money back, but after that, there'd be $18.00 every week till spring. Didn't add that all up, bein' in a hurry to get over to get you."

She made fast annotations. "Five miles a day, to and from, that'd be a far piece for a horse havin' to haul coal all day," Amy pointed out.

"Thought'a that. Thought I'd leave the horses down at the livery stable and ride Brushy down and back."

Amy nodded. "Then I reckon there'd be some of that $18.00 paid out to the livery for the keep of 'em."

"Yeah, have to figure on that bein' no more'n $3.00 a week, me bringin' down the hay and corn to feed 'em."

"Still have $15.00 clear."

Johnny reined Jasper into a narrow lane. "Man with the Clydesdales lives a good piece up this lane."

Finally, the lane gave way to a clearing with a good house and large barn. The horses were tied to a tree in the front yard and a man sat on the porch. He came walking toward them as they drew into the clearing.

"Look at them horses," Johnny directed in a low voice. "Sunshine fair bounces off their backs, them bein' in such good shape."

Amy didn't say anything. Johnny offered a hand to help her from the buggy, which slowed her down only a little. She walked over to the horses, her face without expression. She looked the animals over from all sides and from their hoofs to their ears. The men watched her.

Without a word, she turned and walked to the buggy. She lifted her skirt slightly, stepping on a spoke of the wheel. She eased gracefully over into the buggy and plopped down on the seat. The owner of the horses and Johnny stared after her.

"Come on, Johnny. Take me home," she demanded.

"But, Amy…?"

"Don't talk to me. We gonna get mules and they'll be good enough for what we need. You see if they ain't, and maybe they'll be better for a lot better price."

"But…?"

"You heard me. I don't know why you drug me over here to look at these ugly beasts and me wantin' to get mules."

"But, Amy, you know what I said about gettin' mules."

"And you know what I said. Come take me home."

The man called Johnny to one side. Amy strained her ears to hear him say to Johnny, "See if she'll let you have 'em for $70.00 each."

Johnny shook his head and whispered loudly, "Mister, I ain't never seen this side'a that girl. I reckon if she don't want them horses, we'll be leavin' 'em here."

The man told Johnny, "Now, let's don't be in no hurry."

Amy grinned inwardly and shouted to Johnny, "Come on. I'm tired of waitin' on you. Them horses ain't worth more'n $40.00 each, or maybe $50.00 on their best day."

Johnny turned and walked slowly toward the buggy. The man followed.

"Lady, you let him buy these horses for $50.00 each?"

She put on her best pout and lifted her chin. The dimple could have been carved from stone. "I don't know," she told the man. "That'd be for the harness, too, I reckon? Wouldn't fit nothin' you got left, anyway."

The man looked back at his horses, then at Amy. He nodded. Johnny stared from one to the other.

She continued, "We gonna have us a paper that says they been bought and paid for, all your neighbors knowin' they used to belong to you? Wouldn't want no one to think we stole 'em."

The man nodded, "You write out the paper for whatever it was you said and I'll be goin' after the harnesses."

The man turned to go and Amy began to write on a scrap of paper.

"But Amy?" began Johnny.

"Johnny, don't you say one word to me till we get out'a here."

Johnny was quiet. He took the harnesses and piled them in the floorboard at her feet. He tied the Clydesdales to the rear of the buggy with thick rope and the man wrote his name on the paper. Johnny counted out five $20.00 bills and climbed into the buggy and the man turned and walked toward his house without so much as a goodbye.

Johnny circled the buggy around and started down the lane. He stared soberly ahead. The girl sat primly beside him.

When they reached the road, Amy clapped her hand over her mouth to capture a giggle. Johnny looked at her and grinned. She took her hand from her mouth and laughed and Johnny laughed with her. They laughed together happily, hitting each other's arms in their excitement.

"Amy, how come you to know that man'd sell them horses for $50.00 each, them bein' easy worth $75.00 to me?"

"It weren't no trick. I just looked around. That man has him a nice house and a real big barn, so he ain't needin' money that much. He had mules in the barnyard so as to have somethin' to plow with, and he had one of them fancy little buggies like some women like to ride in, that couldn't be pulled by no big horse. And last thing, just look at them horses and think when they could'a had a day's work, them bein' fat and rested?

"I reckoned that man had 'im a wife, sayin' to 'im, 'You get rid of them beasts 'afore they eat us out'a house and home and don't set your eyes on gettin' no more.'

"And that paper we seen at the courthouse, it had the corners all bent and turned up, like it had been there some time. Likely, there hadn't been too many folks come to look at them horses.

"First time you come to talk to 'im, you was ridin' Brushy, him bein' a good pony, and you was wearin' good clothes, so he says, 'That man'd be able to pay $75.00 each for them horses.' She paused for breathe.

"That's why I thought to do that poutin' and whinin'."

Johnny frowned. "But you didn't tell me what you was fixin' to do. Had me wonderin' what went wrong with you."

"I couldn't'a told you, Johnny. You bein' a man, an honest one at that, you couldn't help but give it all away. Or happen you'd start to laugh and set me off. Now, you got you $50.00 more'n you thought you'd be havin' at this minute."

"Amy Catherine Darnell, if you ain't the beatinest girl I ever seen! I don't know too much for sure, but I do know this one thing. Come time we go to buy our land, you gonna be along with me. Could be, you'll talk 'im into throwin' in two water wells and a coal mine. Maybe get 'em to pay us to take it off their hands."

Johnny reached toward her and she took his hand. They were a quarter of a mile from home. The shiny horses placed their massive hoofs one after the other as they stepped in unison behind the buggy. No ordinary saddle would fit these animals, nor were they bred for riding. Harnessed to a coal wagon, they could work all day with no rest. They could pull a loaded hay wagon up a hill and never break a sweat. The sound of their hoofs behind the wagon was music to Johnny's ears. With these horses behind him and his girl at his side, anything was possible.

While Amy and Johnny were gone, pa had come in from the field and had listened to the amazing story told by his womenfolk. Consequently, he was waiting on the porch when Jasper turned from the road into the driveway, drawing behind the buggy, two magnificent horses, their chestnut manes and tails flowing, and their shiny dark coats glinting in the sun. A fringe of white hairs circled each massive hoof, flouncing like a ruffle with each step.

Amy waved proudly as the buggy circled the driveway for better display of the new animals.

Pa left the porch and came striding toward the gate with mama and Gran coming closely behind. Very few occasions brought Gran farther than her willow rocker.

Johnny, grinning widely enough to fairly split his face, walked over to Amy's pa.

Pa went to the nearest horse, extending his palm to the animal to be sniffed at and blowed upon, rather like saying hello to the animal. "Son, them's two fine lookin' animals. When'd you be needin' a pair? Thinkin' to do a little breedin'?"

Before Johnny could answer, his daughter squealed out, "Oh, pa, we could, couldn't we? I never thought to notice. I was busy lookin' at the house and barn where we got 'em."

"Huh?" wondered Pa, staring at his youngest who had obviously gone daft.

"Yes, sir, Mr. Darnell," Johnny spoke up. "It was Amy a'play actin' that saved us $50.00 off the price of these horses. With her a'talkin', we got 'em for $50.00 each."

"These? Then there must be somethin'..." Pa examined the horses, feeling their legs all the way down to their hoofs. "Hmmm, ain't likely to go lame. Sure came a'prancin' in the yard, proud like."

He lifted the lip of one of the horses. "Young, too. Johnny, boy, 'ppears like you had a gun in your hand, these bein' that much of a steal. Teeth and feet look good. Coats sparklin' so as to blind a body."

"Didn't need me no gun, Mr. Darnell. I had Amy. The man was askin' $75.00 each and I was ready to plunk it down, me wantin' them horses that bad...."

"And you'd'a still had you a bargain."

"I know that."

"Like I asked while back, what you aimin' to do with these animals 'afore they eat you out'a house and home?"

Johnny lifted his chin and raised his voice proudly, so the women could all hear. "I got me a job down in River Bend haulin' coal out'a a seam high on the mountain. Gonna pay me $3.00 a day, could be more later."

Mama and Gran were wide-eyed and properly impressed. Pa was practical. "Son, you got washboard ruts over there on that mountain. Get the weight of a load of coal back'a these animals, be a heavy proposition. Be hard on a horse, even a Clydesdale, holdin' back on a load like that. You or your pa got wagon enough to do it?"

"Gonna buy me a wagon. The coal company got one for sale. Got good brakes on it. Time was, they let the drivers use the wagon for free, but no more. Happen most drivers'd be not as careful with company wagons as they would be of their own. Said they had one driver that up and drove off with their horses and wagon. Took it full'a coal, too. Ain't seen hide nor hair of 'im to this day."

Pa nodded encouragement.

"They say to me, if a man have his own wagon and team, better they pay more for the haulin' than go to the expense of keepin' it up themselves. Said they learned a lesson givin' the job to just whoever come by that said they could drive. Now, they only want a local man as'll be with 'em all winter."

Pa nodded again. "Johnny, your pa ain't got his hay in yet, has he? Likely I could..."

Johnny cut in with assurance, "Thank ya, Mr. Darnell, but this job'a mine ain't gonna start for three weeks, givin' me time to get all that hay in the dry. Wouldn't leave my pa that'a'way, bein' that a lot of what he raised was for my livestock."

Pa nodded with understanding. "Ain't had no luck findin' a place'a your own, yet?"

Amy glanced sidelong at Johnny's face. Johnny never blinked an eye.

"Been doin' me a lot'a thinkin'. I done come to a conclusion, this bein' the one time I got to get exactly what I want for me and Amy. Found it was gonna cost more money than I had on me right now, and so I got me this job. Bein' a good job, it'll let me put cash money away, time the right place comes along."

Amy cut her eyes at Gran and Gran was looking at her. When Gran caught her granddaughter's eyes, she looked away quickly, seeming to study the horses, with her gnarled hand clamped firmly over her mouth. She lay her other hand on mama's arm.

"Essie, honey, you help me back to my chair, will you? Them horses're a sight to look on, but my feet are fair give out on me."

"Sure enough, Gran, I should'a been thinkin' of your feet, 'stead'a listenin' to the men folks."

Mama led Gran back to her rocker. Amy watched with interest. Should she return to the house, too? No, there was mama, coming back toward her.

Johnny talked on. "Way I see it, now'd be the time to be gettin' just the place I want, 'afore a passle'a other problems come in on me. Pa says bad things come in bunches and best to be ready for 'em."

Amy continued to watch, proudly, as Johnny put forth his ideas now to her pa. Johnny was now thinking just the way she wanted him to think, but she did not stop to think how much his thinking had changed in the past few weeks, or how freely he now discussed them.

"Got'a be goin', now," he said, finally. "Bein' gone from home all day, I got chores to catch up on. Speck it might take longer with two new animals to see after."

"Bye, Johnny."

"I'll be ridin' back across the holler little after dark, Amy," he promised.

"Sure."

Johnny urged Jasper into motion and the Clydesdales pranced behind in perfect step, so well was their gait matched. Pa put his arm around mama, and a hand on his daughter's shoulder. "Mama, I speck our little girl made herself a good choice of a man. Think of the luck of havin' him so close. Good thinkin' pa he's got to tell him to work now and get a good place. Made a good buy on them horses, too. Why, a foal dropped out'a that mare'd likely buy a winter bill'a groceries, if it was bein' sold."

Amy had heard enough. She eased around them and walked to the porch where Gran sat, leaving her parents to their own talk.

"Gran, did you think the horses was purty? You hear Johnny's good ideas?"

Gran grinned, her eyes twinkling. "Amy Catherine, honey, what I hear is Johnny's voice sayin' your ideas and you lettin' 'im think they was his."

The girl paused a minute before she corrected, "Your ideas, Gran."

"Now, child, no call to go that far."

Amy knelt beside Gran's rocker and put her arms around the old woman. Gran lovingly stroked the flowing, unruly hair. "You'd be my biggest pleasure left on this earth, Amy Catherine. You call that to mind, happen you think about your old Gran."

Pa and mama were coming back up the walk. Mama announced, "Supper's 'bout on the table. You'all get washed up."

As she followed Gran to the kitchen, Amy's mind raced ahead. Johnny has a job. Three weeks from now he'll be going down there to River bend every day. It was clearly time to go on with the rest of her plan. Three weeks would get the summer canning out of the way, her dresses lengthened and perhaps give her time to devise some way to keep her hair on top of her head. Three weeks.

13

AMY CATHERINE DARNELL stood before the brick facade of the River Bend Mercantile, looking at the massive front of it. The wide, double doors each had a huge plate glass window, and above the doors was a transom with a crank attached for ventilating the building. On either side of the door there was a large display area. One side was taken up with a new cream separator, and two milk buckets. The other side contained a pile of new harnesses in a store-bought watering trough.

Though she had been in the Mercantile many times, everything now seemed totally unfamiliar and that feeling was not caused by her longer dress, her pinned up hair or the fact that she wore her Sunday shoes. What was different was that she had never before asked for a job. In fact, she could not remember ever asking for something of this importance. Not being a town girl, she was not sure Mr. Jenkins would recognize her, and she didn't know if that was good or bad. What she wanted most at this minute, was to turn and run to the livery stable where Johnny had stationed the buggy. If she could just get to Johnny's buggy, she would sit inside and be safe.

Twice, she had forced herself to take a step toward the frightening door. Twice, her mind had told her, 'Just who do you think you are that Mr. Jenkins would give you a job, just like that?"

She swallowed again, but her mouth was dry. She couldn't make a sound. Now, how can you ask for a job if you can't talk? She hurriedly walked the block back to the livery and climbed into the buggy. She had water in a quart fruit jar, so she took a drink and leaned back with relief. This buggy seemed like her home. But she couldn't stay at home. She had already decided that.

Back in front of the Mercantile again, she paused, took one step and then another. She was on the doorstep. Another step and she was inside.

Several customers milled about in the store and Amy pretended to look at something on the counter. Ah, there was Mr. Jenkins over in the corner.

She wandered about looking at this and that. All customers seemed to be occupied. She forced her feet to walk over to the owner.

Mr. Jenkins beamed at her over the tiny glass circles of his spectacles. "What can I do for you, young lady?"

He didn't even recognize her. Maybe that was good. She cleared her throat and started out, bravely. "Mr. Jenkins, I'd like to ask you something."

The old man grinned, tolerantly. "I don't get no profit from talkin', so spit it out."

"I was thinkin' about gettin' me a job, and I was thinkin' this might be a good place to do it."

"Huh?" responded the old man.

"I was thinkin', maybe you have woman customers what'd like to have a woman to sell things to 'em, bein' able to answer questions on how somethin' looks likely better'n a man. If they was to wonder if this piece'a yard goods or that one be better with the color of their hair, I could say which, and say other words to maybe make 'em buy more things."

A frown appeared on the wrinkled brow. "Young lady, I never heard of such impertinenance in my whole born days. You sayin' what

I think I hear you sayin' that you want me to pay you money to say to women that they look good? You must'a been in the sun too long, turned your brain to puddin'." He stared dramatically at the upper corner of the store. "I swear, there's no end to the dumb things I hear comin' out'a woman's mouths. Ain't there things enough at home to keep you busy? Now you get out'a here and let me get on with my work."

Amy felt her eyes filling with tears, blurring her vision. She wanted to turn and run out the door, but she forced her feet to march, one after the other, to the corner of the store where the bolts of yard goods were stacked and piled, unattractively, bolt on bolt, and the whole pile leaning precariously. She felt Mr. Jenkins's eyes following her.

She fingered this fabric and that, and examined the lace wound on spools. Mr. Jenkins strode purposefully toward her. "Told you once to get out'a my store and I ain't doin' it no more. Do I got'a get a broom and chase you out, like a clod'a dirt?"

Amy's eyes were now dry and her voice firm and clear. "Why, whatever do you mean, Mr. Jenkins? You want me to leave here and me a customer? Me and Johnny Scott, who works down at the coal company, we're gonna get married 'afore long, and my Gran, she'd want me to have purty dresses made up by then. I thought to look over what you got here, 'afore goin' on to Jacksonville. Me and Johnny, we was over there last month, but havin' other things to do, there weren't no time to go to see the yard goods. You want me out'a here, reckon he'll just have to take me back to Jacksonville, next time he goes." She paused, noting the surprised look on the man's face.

With a tilt of the head to look up at him, she continued. "You likely know about my Johnny? He drives that little paint pony when he takes me ridin'. 'Course, for work, he takes that matched pair'a Clydesdales he's got. Or I could go over to Jacksonville with my pa, happen he to have crops to sell. 'Course, got no way'a knowin' you ain't got somethin' nice down under this mess. I could gouge around down in there and see, havin' to wait a while for Johnny to take me home."

The old man looked at the girl. Her dress was nice and her fingernails were clean. Her hair seemed to have a problem, but maybe that was the new style. Who was she, anyway?

Amy, bolstered with unexpected courage, chatted on. "I got me five brothers older'n me and every one of 'em got a wife. All them ladies'd want somethin' new to wear to my weddin'. Gran handed my brothers cash money to get nice things for 'em when they got married. Did I tell you I was my Gran's onliest granddaughter? She sets a great store by me, sayin' I'd likely want a lot'a white lacy underthings. I ain't made up my mind, yet. You got any more lace than this? And buttons, you got any? My Gran'd like some more colored thread to embroider for me, like she's doin' this very minute. 'Course, if you want me to be leavin', I'll just walk right out that door. That be what you want, Mr. Jenkins?"

Mr. Jenkins guessed it didn't matter who she was. If she had a grandmother with cash money, and if she was a favorite, there might yet be a profit in there somewhere. And a wedding, she had said.

"You can stay and look through what I have. Got another bolt or two of that yard goods in the back, what I ain't had time to set out. Sneak in the back and take a look, if you're a mind to."

Amy, now in a forgiving spirit, smiled widely at the old man. "Oh, thank you, Mr. Jenkins. Speck I'll be doin' just that."

She arranged the bolts of fabric on their end, and they took up a lot less space. Also, they were in much less danger of falling over. The two bolts in the back room turned out to be ten bolts, and she brought them out and added them to the display. She lined the spools of lace along in front of the fabric, loosening the end of each, so the pattern of the lace could be better seen.

Mr. Jenkins was somewhat apprehensive, but every time he glanced in her direction, she seemed to be studying the effect of the lace over fabric, and all women, he knew, took an eternity to decide what they wanted.

Amy wandered casually to the shoes and boots. She blew the dust from a pair of brown, felt boots, trimmed in leather and velvet. She took the boots to the yard goods and found a wool plaid of the same shade of brown. She took the fabric from the display and set it on the counter with the boots on top. Nice. She sorted through the stockings and found a silky, black pair and draped them across the top of the boots. Hmmmm..

Where were the rest of the stockings? Surely, there would be more than this, with winter coming on.

"Mr. Jenkins, this be all your stockings? I don't see my size and my Gran likes them warm, wool ones like you ain't got many of here."

"That's all of 'em'," he admitted.

Then she began to look at the buttons, all bunched together in a basket. Among them was a card with a pair of garters stretched over it. What garters they were! The elastic was thick and strong. They were bound with shiny blue thread wound around and around, making them smooth as satin.

She took one from the card and tested it for strength, her mind seething with its new idea. She put the garter back on the card and buried it again, deep underneath the buttons. Hunger reminded her it was past lunchtime, so she quietly left the store and went to the livery.

Sitting in the buggy, she ate her bread and butter and the two peaches she had brought for her lunch, topping it off with three chocolate cookies. Water in the jar tasted somewhat like the rubber seal in the lid, but it was wet. Her mind was not on the water, but on the garters. She had brought no money with her, but certainly Johnny would have some. Twenty cents was the price of them. Too much, actually. How would Johnny feel about handing her twenty cents? Well, she'd soon see.

After lunch, she went back. Mr. Jenkins said nothing as she continued to examine and rearrange his wares.

A lady came in and began to look at the yard goods. Amy watched from the corner of her eye. She casually picked up the boots and rearranged them on the brown and green plaid wool. Stepping back, she intoned, "Hmmmm."

The lady looked at Amy, then at the boots.

Amy commented. "Had my money with me today, I'd be gettin' me these here boots and have my Gran make me a skirt with a bustle back. Reckon they'd look good together. Them boots won't be here more'n today, I'd say." She sadly put them back.

She took a few steps away and picked up a bolt of lace, laying it against her arm to study the pattern.

The lady picked up the felt boots and examined them. She looked around and deciding she was not being observed, she tested the boot sole against her own shoe. She slid her hand into the boot, stroking its soft lining, then she stared out the plate glass window, her lower lip caught in her teeth.

Finally, carrying the boots and the bolt of fabric, she signaled to Mr. Jenkins. He was busy at the cream separator display and didn't see her.

Now was the time. Amy spoke up, "Ma'am, you want I cut you a dress length off that?"

The lady startled at the girl's voice, "Why, yes. I didn't know you did that."

"Oh, yes, ma'am. Mr. Jenkins'd be wantin' me to cut this for you. He got hisself busy, over there."

Amy expertly unrolled the bolt, measuring it against the yardstick that had been nailed to the cutting board. As she snipped her way across the fabric with dull scissors, she chatted, "Mr. Jenkins, he got some purty stuff hid down under the counter."

Amy smiled, conspiratorially, "But I know where it is and I could show you."

She reached under the counter and drew out a card of shiny brown buttons and a spool of creamy, crocheted lace. "Only got him one card of these buttons and not much of this lace. Wouldn't had any if it was out here where just anybody could see it. Savin' it for special people, but I knowed you'd be wantin' to see how purty it looks with this yard goods...."

The lady looked at the lace. "I'll take it, too. And the buttons."

She didn't even smile at Amy as she gathered her purchases and went to the cash register to pay for them.

A bent, old woman with a heavily lined face tapped her cane ahead of her as she crept toward the fabric corner. Amy was busily arranging the footwear. She picked up a pair of boots made of smooth leather and a pair of high, button shoes. She examined one, then the other, carefully.

As the old woman neared, Amy commented, "My Gran be gonna need new shoes soon, but I was lookin' at these here boots, thinkin' they'd likely be easier on her calluses." She paused, thoughtfully, then continued.

"Why, lookie here at this soft inside. Feels a mite like baby kitten fur. Her feet get cold of a winter, when she can't be up and around."

The old woman slipped her hand into the boot, as instructed. She agreed they would surely be soft and warm.

"If my Gran had them boots, she'd likely need these here wool stockings. It's the last pair in the store. Be no cold get next to her feet, havin' these on."

The lady who made the first purchase, paused by the door, listening to Amy' chatter.

The old woman fingered the wool stocking, then slipped her hand inside. They indeed felt warm and cozy against her memory of the cold of winter.

"Child, you done talked me into thinkin' a winter. Can't always get stockings here just 'cause you happen to be needin' 'em. Now, lookie, what you got me doin'? Come in here to pick up a card'a buttons and you got me buyin' stockin's."

Amy smiled her friendliest smile. "I was just sortin' out them buttons. You'll get to make first choice. You bring along a piece'a somethin' to match?"

The woman brought from her apron pocket, a scrap of pink fabric. She grinned, toothlessly, at Amy. "Makin' up wrappers for my granddaughter's new baby. Girl, it was. Got herself a little girl."

Amy picked several cards of small, pink buttons and one card of white shiny ones, holding the scrap against each card. The woman chose the white buttons, the soft boots and the pair of wool stocking. Amy heard her repeating to Mr. Jenkins how the helpful young lady had talked her into buying the boots, seeming to know they would feel good because of her having a Gran to think about.

Mr. Jenkins made no response.

Amy had all the footwear dusted and setting in a row when Johnny came for her. He was black from coal dust and stood politely near the outside door. Amy hurried toward him, her knot of hair sliding lower over her left ear.

"Johnny, I need to have twenty cents to buy somethin'."

Without hesitation or comment, Johnny produced two dimes and Amy extracted the blue garters from their hiding place and gave Mr. Jenkins the money.

"Mr. Jenkins, I'd call it a shame I didn't have the time to see all you got. Happen I'll be back soon."

In the buggy, she proudly displayed the blue garters.

"Got me somethin' now, gonna hold all my hair up where it ought'a stay and not come fallin' down in my face."

Johnny was yet to be convinced. "Think so? Did old man Jenkins have any other pretty things you want? You could look around and see. I still got that money you saved me on them horses."

"Johnny, that money's like any other money you got and it needs to be saved for what we want. You was thoughtful to say that to me, but that's how I feel. I didn't get me no job, yet, but I'm a'goin' back tomorrow."

14

MR. JENKINS SLID back his chair back from the supper table. One thing about Mrs. Jenkins, she could set a good table. Belching contentedly after his fried pork chops, creamed peas and potatoes, fried onions and a desert of steamed pudding, he picked up the Jacksonville Democrat for a pleasant evening of reading.

Mrs. Jenkins had been fidgety all through the meal, but since her husband did not permit conversation while he ate, she was forced to wait until the meal was over to express her mind.

Finally free to talk, she began, "Mr. Jenkins, how much money you payin' that girl to talk to your customers down at the store?"

"Now, Emma, I told you time and time again, that store weren't no worry of yourn. I done took care of that girl." He noisily opened the newspaper, thereby dismissing her.

She would not be so easily dismissed. "I know you always thought I was too dumb to talk to, but I ain't so dumb and I can tell you this much, Mr. Jenkins. You better be payin' that girl a'plenty or you gonna loose her. Miz Markham, over at the pharmacy, been sayin' she gonna find out what that girl's gettin'. Gonna make Mr. Markham go talk to her and tell her he'll pay more if she can come and talk to his customers. Happen you don't want to listen to me, that's up to you but if you don't listen, you gonna be sorry."

Mr. Jenkins did not register the fact that he heard her every word but his eyes refused to focus on the paper before him. He had already been thinking of the two large sales from the women's corner and the sale of the expensive garters that had been in the store for months. Who'd have thought that dusty young man would pay twenty cents for garters for a girl who had already promised to marry him? He noticed, too, that there seemed to be more room in the woman's corner. There seemed to be space for them to walk around, now, not that he had actually walked over there to check it out.

Mrs. Jenkins' voice came threateningly clear as she removed the dishes from the table.

"You think there be nothin' I know, but this is one thing I can tell you. If you let them Markham's take her away from you, like they gonna, you got nothin' to blame it on, 'cept your own pigheadedness."

It was then that Mr. Jenkins knew for certain he had to talk with that girl who had the strange hair that seemed to slide to one side. Who was she, anyway? Boy friend works at the coal company. That'd be how he'd find her.

Before reaching home, Amy had decided not to go back tomorrow. The next day would be soon enough. She was lonesome, now, eager for company, but she had told Johnny she was too tired for him to come over to see her because she had seen how exhausted he was.

Now, in her bed at last, she buried her face in her pillow to smother the sobs. She had really messed up today, and no matter how many days she went in there, Mr. Jenkins would never give her the job. She was a failure. After all that bragging she had done to Gran, she hadn't been successful at all. It was clear that Mr. Jenkins thought he didn't need her. She was right to decide not to go back to morrow. She would stay home and work on the quilt with Gran. They could make a good time of it. Gran would like that. Finally, she slept.

She awoke depressed and dispirited, until she remembered the garters. She dressed hurriedly and, at the washstand, she leaned over and, practically standing on her head, she brushed her hair. The ends of it swept the floor. When it was smooth and shiny, she gathered it together and wound the garter around it, once, then again. She let go with her hands and the top knot was solid. She stood up and hair flowed from the top of her head down in all directions, just like a fountain

Reaching up, she gathered the of taffy candy. The screen of hair hid her grin of triumph. hair in both hands, twisting it softly. She draped the loose coils around the blue garter, completely hiding it. Using small hairpins, she tacked the coil smoothly to her head. The lighter, sun-bleached ends of hair lay in scallops over the darker hair from nearer the roots. The blend of shades accentuated the pulled-taffy candy effect.

Amy held her breath in anticipation as she prepared to look into the wash stand mirror. Pleasant surprise caught her at the pit of her empty stomach, causing mild nausea. She sat down until it passed, then went back to her room and sat on her bed. Had she really done right to give up on the job so easily? Success with the hair created new possibilities. She'd try again. Maybe tomorrow.

Her reverie was interrupted when she heard the separator droning from the kitchen. Her job. Pa must be doing it. The family was already preparing to do without her. She hurried to the kitchen.

Pa was at the separator, but he turned loose of the handle. Mama stared at Amy, forgetting to turn the eggs. Gran held the cup of tea in mid air, not noticing the thin stream of liquid spilling onto the table.

Mama recovered first. "Amy, honey, how did you get your hair up there like that?"

Amy grinned, "Got me a fancy garter underneath, holdin' it up. Johnny bought 'em for me. Gonna wear it all day and see if it stays up. Feels solid, and the pins don't stick me no more."

Gran recovered. "Honey, hand me a tea towel to clean up my mess. Sakes, if you don't look to be a foot taller. Don't she, Essie?"

Pa made no comment. He just shook his head and sighed.

Later, Amy admitted to Gran. "I'm thinkin' it might not be so easy gettin' Mr. Jenkins to hire me. Seems he thinks he don't need no help."

But Gran responded, "Then he'd be the looser, for sure. But here's how it'll be for you. If you find you ain't gettin' what you thought you'd get, then it'd be that somethin' better is bein' planned by the Good Lord. See if it don't work that'a'way. He saw yesterday how things weren't workin' right, so today He'll be tendin' to it. Most likely everything gonna be fixed by tomorrow when you go back."

Mr. Jenkins had watched the door all day. No strange young lady. In the late afternoon, he swallowed his pride and walked down to the River Bend Coal Company.

"Tell that young driver of your, Johnny Scott, to be stoppin' by the Mercantile on his way home, will you?"

The dusty, puzzled Johnny was reluctant to take his coal dust into the store, but Mr. Jenkins waved him on.

"Young fellow," he began, without ceremony, "You gonna see that young lady'a yours today? Well, you tell her to come on back down here and we'll talk about what she asked."

Johnny sensed a change in the attitude of the stern-faced man. "What was it she asked, if you don't mind my askin', Mr. Jenkins?"

"She says if she can stay here and talk with women customers, happen they'll buy more. She thinks a man'd not have the answers to their questions."

Johnny nodded his coal-dusty head. "She'd likely be right on that, Mr. Jenkins. I'll tell her what you said, and if she'd still of a notion to work, I'll bring her back down. 'Course, she won't be stayin' here long. We'll be gettin' married after Christmas."

"Well, you bring her on in."

"Sure, Mr. Jenkins. I'll tell her and see what she says."

Johnny heaved himself into the saddle and urged Brushy forward. As the little paint pony moved along, Johnny shook his head in puzzlement. Amy must have done better than she thought, yesterday. Another thing he noticed, riding this saddle pony had seemed like the practical thing to do, him a man alone, but it was a lot easier for a tired man to sit back in the buggy and rest. Riding home with Amy beside him, talking about this and that, would be something to look forward to at the end of the day. Freighting coal was not an easy job.

15

MUCH LATER, AMY smiled into her pillow and thought, "Gran was right, seems to me. Them people in the town already know about my Johnny 'cause of me, and us not even married. Everybody gonna know my Johnny when they see me standin' there, lookin' purty, talkin' to them town ladies. Someone gonna say, "Who is she and where'd she come from?" And someone else gonna say, "Oh, that'd be the girl gonna marry Johnny Scott. You know Johnny, the fellow workin' that team'a Clydesdales over at the Coal Company.' Yes, Gran was right sayin' we was to give the Good Lord a day to work things out. Happened just like she said."

Before daylight, Johnny was at the Darnell gate with the buggy. Brushy was frisky in the cool of the morning, snorting and jingling his harness.

Amy was waiting on the porch, lunch basket in one hand and skirt tail in the other. It wouldn't do to show up at the Mercantile with dew and grass stains on her dress tail. Today, she wore a summery Sunday dress of deep rose with white dots. It had a wide white collar and the sleeves were puffed and starched stiff. The starch of the sleeves itched a bit on her arms, but it seemed a small price to pay for the way it made her look. A white ruffle had lengthened it acceptably.

There was no worry with her hair. It was as solid as if it had been glued into place, while still managing to look soft and sculptured. A sudden jerk of the head shook not one hair out of place.

Johnny was momentarily taken back by the impressive pile of hair on her head. Surely, the weight of it would give her a headache, but he was forced to concede she had made good use of the twenty-cent garters.

Mr. Jenkins ignored his insults of yesterday. "I been thinkin', it might be a good thing for you to stay here and talk with the women. Happen you could answer their questions good or better'n me. Figure it'd be worth a dollar a day to me."

Amy caught her breath. A dollar every day, just for talking, that being one of the easiest things she ever did. Six dollars every week! She was speechless.

Mr. Jenkins should have let well enough alone, but the memory of the Markhams and Mrs. Jenkins' warning, he continued, "We'll make that be a dollar and ten cents every day."

Amy waited a respectable moment before saying, "All right, Mr. Jenkins. We can do that to start. Happen you see I ain't worth that much, you tell me and I'll give you some back. Then happen you think I might be worth more'n that to you, I know you'll want to give it to me. Wouldn't want it said by no one that you was cheated by me." She flashed a wide, friendly smile and retreated to the women's corner. Today, it would be rearranged in earnest.

She re-grouped the fabric, lighter colors together and darker ones apart. She took hats from their boxes under the counter, fluffing up their crumpled feathers and lace, and dusted their flowers and fruit. She swept the floor of her corner, and, finding no place to stop, swept the entire store.

It was a week or so later, when there were no customers in the store, that she said, "Mr. Jenkins, when my pa or some man wants hisself a store bought harness, he goes in the store and says to give him one. He don't need to be lookin' in no store window to see what they look like, 'cause he already knows. But if my Gran or my mama was to come in the store wantin' a card of buttons, she'd maybe look in the window and see one of them purty hats and say, "Lookie at that! That'd be the hat to go with my Sunday dress." Don't you think that might happen?"

Mr. Jenkins stroked his chin and took the harnesses to the back store room, muttering, "If that chatterbox thinks she can make me take the cream separator out'a the other window, she got another think a'comin'." A man must maintain some pride.

Amy swept out the platform behind the plate glass window and scrubbed the glass inside and out until it sparkled. She took a bolt of flowered fabric and spread it in ripples on the floor of the platform. She selected a pair of shiny, patent leather pumps and a spool of black ribbon. Stockings would be nice, but there were none in the store. There was a hat with flowers and a pair of lace gloves. She found a silver-looking hair brush and a mirror to match so she put them in the window and went out to the sidewalk to check the effect. No, the brush and mirror would have to go. They were too shiny to match the colors of the other things.

Ladies going by on the brick sidewalk stopped to stare at the display. Several of them came in for a better look. Some looked at the display and others studied the girl.

One nicely dressed lady whispered to Amy, "Not meanin' to be nosy, honey, but how is it you make your hair stand up so purty, like you do?"

Amy whispered her answer and the lady smiled. Then she wanted to see the garters.

"Oh, we don't have no more, right now. Mr. Jenkins'd likely try to order more, if you want."

"Oh, I wouldn't want to talk to him. Wouldn't be proper, me talkin' to him about garters."

Amy nodded. "You'd be right. That's my job. Come see if we don't have some in a week or two."

At lunchtime, she hurried to the livery and climbed into the buggy. She studied spelling words as she ate her lunch. Why couldn't words be spelled the way they sounded? She dreaded to start the English Composition. Mr. Campbell had warned her that her people had their own way of putting sentences together that, while being easily understood, did not necessarily agree with the book. Strange, the way the book made things harder than they ought to be.

The mild weather of September and October made the trip home restfully pleasant. Most evenings found Amy cuddled against the side of the buggy with the speller or the English book in front of her. Johnny, oftener than not, would be leaning against the other side of the seat with his head back, and his eyes closed, allowing Brushy to find his own way.

By late October, however, there was hardly enough light for her to see to read in the evenings, and the shortness of the day meant total darkness in the morning. With November came the unpleasant weather. The wind and rain made the oilskin flaps necessary and the roads were so sticky and gummy, the small pony was hard put to keep the buggy in the road without constant help from Johnny on the brake. The extra hour in the dark made a long-seeming day and by evening, they were both exhausted.

"Amy, how long you thinkin' to keep on workin'?"

"Hadn't thought on it. Why?"

"Don't reckon you ought'a be out in this weather, come winter. Won't do me no good, neither. Somethin' we got'a consider."

Amy nodded, understandingly. "If I was to quit, what would you do to make the trip shorter?"

"Somethin', maybe"

"Well, truth is, I was thinkin' to find me a place to stay in town. This trip seems to get longer and colder and I get home too late to be of a help to anyone. Just sleep and get up and come back. Miz Jenkins said her sister got a room she'd let out in return for some help. I didn't say nothin' about it, 'afore. That'd' a left you comin' and goin' alone. What would you do?"

"Be no problem to me. I'd stay in the livery with my wagon. It's big as a house, and I'd put me a tent in there and be fine. Could get meals down at the boardin' house or the cafe."

So Amy checked on the room. What duties would she be needing to do in return for it? "Oh, no, honey. Wouldn't want you for no chores. It'd be my husband's mama that's with us. Much as we love her, we been tied to this house for what seems like years. If we was to have a body here to sit of an evenin' and on Sunday morning, it'd give me a chance to visit sometimes and go to the Lord's house once a week. It'd be such a pleasure to get out. Now, there'd be a room for you and meals, and a courtin' parlor if your young man can come over."

She continued. "Heard talk that you had an old Gran, so as you'd know about old people. Some young folks don't understand and I wouldn't be lettin' just anyone stay with her."

Amy moved in with the Thomason's and Johnny into his wagon. Darkness fell so early that the girl found herself studying by candlelight, and Johnny, with winter bringing greater demand for coal, worked later and later and seemed unable to drag himself the two blocks it would be, just for the pleasure of watching her study.

It was hardest on Gran. Lonely tears filled her eyes and she was forced to live on memories. There was no Amy Catherine beside her, filling her mind with thoughts. There was no one needing to hear her own thoughts, anymore. The quilt was finished and still the daisy was the only decoration in the center block. A ring should have been there by now.

"Lord, it ain't for me to be tellin' You about our little girl, You knowin' her already. You been seein' her doin' her best by You and that Johnny. I got this quilt done, bein' the onliest way to leave my words here with her, so if You're thinkin' she don't need me no more, and she ain't gonna be here for me to look at, then the next thing I look for is to be up there with You. Ain't meanin' to hurry You, though. You got enough to do 'thout folks tellin' You what to do."

A tear rolled down the withered cheek, following a wrinkle. It dropped from her chin, unnoticed. Her sweet Amy Catherine would be home on a Sunday in late November. She had promised. Gran needed to stay here that long.

"Right after that, Lord. I'd be ready any time after that."

The River Bend Mercantile looked a lot different from how it had a few months ago. The cream separator had left the other window and a row of lace spools now wore hats of wool and felt and straw, and they were feathered, veiled, made of lace and trimmed in velvet. The silver hair brush and mirror had been sold, and now a gold colored one was in its place. Several handbags were grouped to one side. The change in merchandise had been Mr. Jenkins' idea.

As usual, the residents of River Bend had waited until fall to restock their coal bins. Load after exhausting load came out of the mountain, over the precarious trail, and down into town. Some loads went directly to customers. Residents of River Bend, great and small, met Johnny, the friendly, dusty coal hauler. Occasionally, a woman would say to him, "You'll be the man that knows Amy, down at the Mercantile. She was a big help to me when I was down there. She says to me she'd gonna marry Johnny Scott and I figure that to be you. She's a fine girl, she is."

Johnny would smile through his coal dust. "That'd be my Amy, for sure."

They hardly saw each other at all between Johnny's exhaustion and Amy's studies. What had happened to those long, lazy days of summer and the cool, friendly weekends?

Mr. Jenkins said that perhaps Amy was now worth $1.50 a day. He had told her of that, immediately after she and Mrs. Markham had spent some minutes whispering together over whether the veil of a hat hung just right. The girl had agreed that the veil had a strange hang to it, and recommended she get a length of lace and replace the veil all together. It would make the hat seem to be a new one. The fancy lace for the veil cost forty cents.

The River Bend Coal Company decided Johnny was worth $3.50 a day, and two weeks later, they decided it should be $4.00. The money was a welcome means to an end, but it didn't help the cold loneliness. What happened to the fun of last summer? The wonderful sunshine? The sweat and dust of his pa's farm and the trips to see Amy in the evening? Where were they, now, and how did he get so tired?

Together, they were saving at least $20.00 a week. It was a lot more than they had thought they would have, but thinking of the months ahead was just too exhausting. Something was dreadfully wrong with this plan, but Johnny was too tired to figure out what.

16

GRAN FELT THE heaviness in her chest before she opened her eyes. She knew what it was, but she felt no fear.

"Lord, I asked You for the seein' of my little Amy Catherine one more time, and I thank You for that. My little girl was so beautiful and full of happy words, I wouldn't'a wanted to take that from her. She ain't got that ring, yet, but it don't seem to be worryin' her none. Speck she knows what she's doin'."

Gran shifted under her warm quilts, seeking a position that would let her breathe easier. In her mind, she played back the wonderful Sunday. It had been a family holiday. Two of her own sons were there. Strong, wonderful men. Two out of three was better than just one out of three, and she must be thankful.

The grandsons, all of them married to fine girls, were there. Small children, so many she had difficulty remembering who they belonged to. Beautiful children, pink cheeked and laughing and they were hers, just as if she had given birth to them herself. Essie's littlest boy would have his own baby by Christmas. That left only Amy Catherine.

"Rather wanted to be here, Lord, and see my little girl at the alter. Times she put me in the mind of yellow butterflies, she did, flittin' here and there after whatever was good. You been good to me, Lord, and I reckon You'll see her through that weddin' 'thout me."

The heaviness in Gran's chest was now punctuated by a small pain. Small, but sharp.

The door opened.

"How you feelin', Gran? Gonna be able to eat some breakfast?"

Essie's cheerful voice cut through her thoughts. She made herself smile. "Think I might lay here a mite longer, Essie."

"You sick, Gran? What's wrong?" Essie rushed to the bed. Her cool hand tested Gran's brow. "Fever. That's what you got. You stay right there and rest. I got your tea ready and you can have it right here in the bed." Then Essie was gone.

Gran closed her eyes. "Lord, did I 'member to thank You for Essie? That girl took good care'a my boy and me and she let me have time with her sweet Amy Catherine, just like she was my own. Lord, of all them things You give me, Essie'd be right up there with whatever's on top."

Essie was back with the tea. She plumped the pillows and propped Gran's bent body carefully into position. "You want I sit with you, Gran? Or you think you can rest?"

"Don't you fret, Essie. I'll be fine. I'll just rest here and drink my tea. It's good tea, Essie, honey. You always did make the best tea."

Essie paused a moment, looking at Gran, then she turned quietly and left.

It was mid morning the next day that Amy saw her pa coming through the door of the Mercantile. One look at his face drove daggers into her stomach and filled her eyes.

"Pa?"

He looked at her with helpless misery in his eyes. He held out his arms to her and she walked into them. It was that action that told Amy that her fears were true.

She whispered, "It'd Gran. I know its Gran. Is she...?"

"She's alive, or she was when I left. She's askin' to have you brought up in a hurry."

Mr. Jenkins rushed her out, promising to explain to his sister-in-law where she went. The climb into the mountains was long, cold and quiet. What was there to say?

"Pa, you say anything to Johnny?"

Pa nodded. "Folks at the coal company gonna tell 'im, once he drives in."

The driveway in front of the house was packed with wagons and buggies. The brothers and their families had already gathered in, and their children wandered about, forlorn and puzzled. Adults stood in groups, discussing things of no importance.

Amy let pa help her out of the buggy, seeming to wish to prolong entry into the house, yet her heart beat against her chest in dreaded anticipation.

The door opened for her and her family stood aside for her to be ushered into Gran's bedroom.

She heard mama say, "Gran, we brung Amy Catherine to you. We got her right here." Mama paused a minute, then closed the door, leaving the girl alone with Gran.

"Gran?"

A weak voice answered, "Honey, come lean over me."

Gran fumbled her fevered hand from under the quilt covering, and took Amy's cold one. Into the girl's hand she pressed a hard, warm object, closing the chilly's fingers over it.

Amy burst into tears. "No, Gran, not your beast pin. I don't want it. You keep it. You'll be wantin' to wear it, time you get well." But Gran's hot, weak fingers held Amy's hand closed.

"No, honey, I pray hard for your pa to hurry, bringin' you here. Hankered to be puttin' that breast pin in your hand myself. Weren't much time left."

"No, Gran, don't leave me. You ain't told me everything. You ain't made my ring block. You got'a stay."

Gran's voice was faint. "Amy Catherine, honey, you gonna make that ring block. I done all the rest and that's gonna be left for you to do. You got'a use that shiny thread and be neat in your stitchin'."

"No, Gran, I can't. I won't," the anguished girl wailed. "Don't leave me, Gran."

"Hush, honey. You doin' fine. Ask your mama about the paper I been savin' for you. You mama knows all about it." Gran's voice was very low and hesitant. Amy leaned her ear to Gran's face to catch every word.

"Amy Catherine, honey?"

"What, Gran?"

There was no answer.

"Gran?"

A hesitation. "I tell you…"

"Tell me what, Gran?"

"I was gonna tell you, you an Johnny… come springtime……" The voice was a faint whisper.

"Gran, what was it? Say what you was gonna tell me? Please, Gran, don't go away. Take me with you, Gran."

The frail, hot hand fell away from Amy's cold ones and lay limply on the bedclothes.

"Gran? GRAN!"

The faint rise and fall under the quilt was gone. The girl's sobs shook the bed and her tears fell on Gran's withered cheek.

"Mama!' she wailed. "Pa!"

The door opened and a steam of light from the oil lamp fell across the bed. "Pa, Mama, Gran left me!" Her tear-stained face looked toward her pa, standing silently with his arms stretched toward her once more. Tears streamed down his face. She had never seen tears like those in her pa's eyes and the sight of them melted her very heart. She ran to him, falling into his arms and sobbing on his shoulders. She felt the warmth of mama's arms around them both. Her brothers came, one by one, touching, holding, drawing together, and the first pain of their loss passed over them. Choking sobs punctuated Amy's wails, tearing her breath to ragged gasps.

"Mama, Gran was a'sayin' somethin' to me and she left 'afore it was said. Gran was tellin' me somethin' and I want her to come back and tell me what it was."

One by one, the brothers melted away, leaving Mama with her arms around her daughter. "I know, Amy, honey. I know. There don't come no time that we'd be ready to let Gran go. Gran had to go when the Good Lord knowed it was time. What you got in your hand, honey?"

Amy opened her hand. There was Gran's breast pin, the metal filigree creating a dented imprint in her palm.

"See what you got there? Last thing a'worryin' Gran was if you was gonna get here so she could put that breast pin in your hand. She said it was a'usin' up her strength, wantin' you to be here 'afore she left."

"Mama, I don't want this here breast pin. I want Gran."

"I know, Amy, child, but that pin is the part of Gran that'll not be gettin' old and tired. That'd be a special part and parcel of Gran, and her givin' it to you showed she died a'thinkin' of you. Some things we get to hold in our hands and other things we hold in our hearts. Gran gave you both of them things."

Eventually Amy's sobs quieted, and she looked at the yellow stone shining up from her palm. Its color reflected the light from the oil lamps.

Mama continued with comforting words. "Gran said she wanted me to take her willow rocker and think about her time and again, while I was restin'. She said auntie was to have her sewin' basket and all them colored threads, 'cept for the shiny yellow that was for the finishin' of your quilt. Then she said the breast pin was to be give to you, happen you didn't get here...."

"Mama, I changed my mind. I want this here breast pin."

"You're a good girl. You gonna be fine." Mama gently led Amy into the room where the family had gathered. Faces glanced at her tear-stained and reddened face and turned away, discretely, conveying their sympathy.

There was a knock at the door. The preacher stood there, hands extended, flanked by his wife and two ladies from the church.

"We come to sit up with you folks. No words can say....."

The house filled with people. Amy stood looking at the yellow stone in her hand. No one noticed her as she stepped out on the porch and sat down in Gran's rocker. It was past eleven o'clock when the Clydesdales trudged, exhausted, into the drive.

Dave took the reins and led them to the warm corral and the feed box, and Johnny ran to the porch. He saw her alone in the wicker rocker, huddled into a dejected heap. He knelt beside her and held her ice-cold hands.

"Johnny, Gran's gone," she said, dully.

"I know. Dave told me."

"I can't make it without Gran."

"Sure you can, honey. You got me."

"Johnny, Gran's last words was about us. She said things about you and me in the springtime, but she didn't say what."

"Gran was likely sayin' that you and me, we'd have each other, come springtime, and we was to remember that when we felt tired and lonely. You think that'd be somethin' Gran'd say?"

The girl nodded.

"Amy, you got fingers like icicles. No wonder, sittin' out here in this weather. I got'a take you inside."

Somehow they made it through the night. The men retired to the warmth of the hay barn, sleeping in shifts. The children were bedded down on the floor, and the women made pots of coffee and rested where they could. People talked of this and that, giving the family something to do, so they wouldn't have to think.

Morning came and the men made a pine box out in the barn. They brought it into the parlor and the women lined it with a snow-white sheet. They put in a pillow encased in a freshly ironed pillowcase. Gran wore her best Sunday dress, and appeared to be napping in the box.

Johnny did not leave for work. Amy asked him why. "Told 'em I had to go to my girl, 'cause she needed me. Wasn't feared to loose my job, 'cause where'd they be gettin' a man with a rig and team that'd do what I do, here at the comin' of winter? Happen they do, I'll just find another job, just like I found that'n. Some things just naturally comes before other things."

Johnny scrubbed the coal dust from the huge wagon and brushed the Clydesdales until they shone. Gran took her last ride behind their prancing, high stepping gait. It had begun to snow huge flakes, but Amy sat beside Johnny as he drove them to the white wooden church beside the cemetery.

The minister spoke in pleasant tones but she could not focus on the words. Then she was standing beside the box. Her mother stood on one side of her and Johnny on the other. Johnny held her arm, comfortingly.

Gran looked exactly as though she had just fallen asleep. This is wrong, Amy told herself. We should take her home. She reached one hand into the pine box and touched Gran's hand with her forefinger. No, they were right. Gran was gone. What looked like Gran was not Gran, at all!

Johnny led her away, out of the church and to the wagon. Flakes of snow had covered the exposed seat and Johnny brushed them away. He spread a warm quilt around them both, turned the team and left in the opposite direction of the Darnell house. Down the backside of Five-Mile-Hill they rode, past farm houses and barns.

Snow settled in the pines and cedars and made the road white, for, after all, it was December.

"Johnny, I can't go on alone. Gran's gone."

"I know you can't go on alone, Amy, and Gran knew it, too. We don't have to go on alone 'cause we have each other."

The girl nodded, gratefully.

Johnny turned the horses around and climbed back up the hill. A dusting of snow covered their heads and the quilt, but their faces were warm and rosy. It was time to go home.

Everyone else had left the Darnell house, and finally Johnny drove away with the Clydesdales. "I'll be comin' back for you Sunday, Amy. I'll have Brushy and the buggy." Then it was quiet.

17

AMY WANDERED FROM room to room, wishing for Sunday and the return to the Mercantile. She wished for the hats and shoes and the bolts of yard goods. For the buttons, the lace and the garters. She did not want to look at the empty willow rocker.

It was then that Mama remembered, "Amy, honey, there'd be that paper for you that Gran wanted you to have. I got it here."

It was a white envelope, somewhat dog-eared at the corners. In the upper left hand corner was printed "Jacksonville Bank".

Amy opened the gummed flap and read,

"For Miss Amy Catherine Darnell:

"I am writing this for your grandmother, Amy, because she asked me to do her a favor. Right now, you're just a little girl, but when you read this, you may be much older.

"When your grandmother, Mrs. Catherine Darnell, sold her land, the parcel west of River Bend, she couldn't bear to give up one certain part of it. It is the strip of land between the road and the river, a parcel of approximately 18 acres in all. It measures 1700 feet along the river and 300 to 500 feet wide.

"She has deposited in my bank enough money to pay the taxes on this land for a number of years and I have been keeping them paid in memory of her husband, your grandfather, who was my close friend. This land belongs to you and I am holding all the papers you need to claim it. There is also a sum of money left from the deposit she made.

As soon as you read this letter, you may come and claim your inheritance. It gave your grandmother much pleasure to help your brothers and your cousins when they needed her, but this, her favorite legacy, was left for you.

"I trust we will see you soon. Yours respectfully, Cecil Coddington, Jacksonville, Arkansas."

Amy looked questioningly into her mama's eyes. "Mama, Gran didn't sell all her land, like we thought. She held back a piece and she says here she was a'savin' it or me. You know what, mama? Johnny and me, we stopped on that very land on the way back from gettin' my schoolbooks. We sat in the grass and Johnny walked over to the river. It was always gonna be mine and Gran kept the secret in her head. I got'a go down and see it."

"Sure, honey. Johnny gonna be here Sunday and there'll be time in the afternoon to go down. Likely pa and Johnny's Pa'd like to ride along."

Pa read the letter. "That'd be Gran, dead out. I knowed about this, but never saw the actual words. Never was a time when somethin' was needed that Gran couldn't find it, whatever it was. Happen you was hungry, she had food, or thirsty, and she had water in a fruit jar. Now Amy's got her that strip of river land. That'd be Gran."`

19

THEN IT WAS Sunday afternoon and the dark, rolling clouds were spitting a freezing mist and it blew in swirls and eddies, biting cheeks and fingers and making eyes water. The windy bluster ripped and tore at their clothing as Amy, Johnny, Mr. Scott and Mr. Darnell stood on the bank of the Tuscalara River, staring into its rolling, swirling depth.

The main body of the water came coursing down the river channel, through Jacksonville, continuing on down the wide valley to the town of River Bend. Being at crest depth, it carried dead leaves and sticks in the foam. A mile to the west it was joined by the rushing War Eagle River, a wild river crashing out of the mountains. Other debris was caught, swirling, from off the banks and carried along for a way, only to be wedged against exposed roots or a downed tree farther down stream.

As the force of the current neared River Bend, it came in contact with the concrete abutments set by the Mississippi Central Railway as a base for their trestle bridge. At this point, only the concrete base of the bridge was in place, but it had already made its presence felt. The water of the river slammed forcefully against the abutment near the southern side of the river, causing a white-water crest to rise above the surface of the water like a furrow of sod behind a plow. This crest curled over and aimed for the opposite bank, carrying with it an accumulation of floating objects. A sheet of ripples was created which crossed the natural flow of the water. Even brimming full, as the river was now, a checkered pattern was created by the crossing of ripple action.

The point on the opposite bank that was affected by the white-water crest was scoured and gouged into a deep pool. A strong stand of willows caught the current and turned it back, only to have it strike against the rock cliff, and be turned again toward the injured bank.

The young couple stood together, staring at the water while the older men walked up and down the bank, discussing the problem.

"The trouble commences with the railroad trestle. Weren't nothin' eatin' at the bank till that was put there. The flow'a that water stood for years, till the railroad people commenced foolin' with the natural river bed."

"That's the truth. Two places need lookin' after 'afore the rest."

"Yep, this'n here and then on down past the willow trees."

"Sad sight. Bad thing to happen to the youngens."

"Yep, got 'em a job'a work ahead, any way you look at it."

"Lookie at the color'a that water. Fair gougin' the soil out from under the bank." Mr. Scott touched the dry grass of the bank with his toe, and a square foot of soil dropped into the water and went barreling away, end over end, following the checkerboard ripples.

"Would you look at that! None too soon to be takin' care of this little problem."

"Look at that log, a'comin' down on the tide."

The lower, root portion of a felled tree came through the rapids, bucking and dipping with the current. With a crash, it slammed against the concrete and pitched away, swirling a crest of foam toward the bank where the men stood.

"Look at it come!"

The log aimed its jagged point against the soft, black dirt of the bank, ramming deep into the mud. It hung, momentarily motionless, then rolling over, it drilled another clod of black soil from the bank, carrying it to the midstream.

"Did you look at that! That'd be just what I allowed been happenin'."

"Them youngens gonna have to do somethin' purty tolerable quick, if they's to be any dirt left here to be stood on."

"You'd be right sayin' that. Reckon we could take a walk down stream and figure what's to be done first."

"Shore wisht I had some time to be helpin' on this problem. Got myself tied down with livestock, right now, lot of 'em Johnny's. Don't want Johnny to think I got too much on me or he'd feel bad. He don't need no more on 'im right now. If it weren't for them cows, I'd find time to haul 'im some rocks down here."

Amy's father nodded agreeably. "Could be I could help you, there. My boys done took their stock away and I got barn and hay enough to care for me and half the county. Run Johnny's animals 'crost the hollow and I'll be puttin' 'em up till he gets ready for 'em."

Mr. Scott turned to Mr. Darnell. "If you was to see your way clear to do that, I'd be down here with the mules and a slip shovel and work on turnin' this river."

"Be no bother to me. Likely, I could help, too, from time to time, on the diggin'."

"Got enough hay, you say?"

"More'n enough."

Johnny and Amy stood apart from the men and the roar of the water that drowned out their words. From the glances their way, it would have been impossible to miss the subject of their conversation.

"Amy, standin' here lookin' in this water, puts me in the mind'a last summer, standin' on this same spot, watchin' the top soil wash away. Look at my pa and your pa standin' over there talkin' it all over, like we wasn't even here, the way a pa does at times, thinkin' his boy got no sense. They mean good, though, and I ain't sayin' they don't.

"But I stand here knowin' a problem when I see one and I know how it's gonna get took care of. See out there where the big rock sticks up? That's where I make out the edge of your land to be. I see I got me a job gettin' the water out and the soil back in."

"You?"

"Yeah, me. That old river been nibblin' away at your land and done took too much. This cut just come on after the railroad commenced to build them pillars, so it ain't cut as deep as it'd be soon. I judge from here out, maybe, eighty or a hunnerd feet, the water'd be two, maybe three, feet deep. Seems from the swirl of the water to have four main eddy holes. Fillin' 'em in gonna take time and I ain't fooled on that."

"But, Johnny...."

"Lookie down there, Amy, at that purty dirt. Ain't nothin' won't grow on this here land. Gonna have land here to grow anything we need, you and me. This here is land. It don't disappear by itself. Once there was dirt all the way out to that flat rock, and that dirt is still someplace. So I know that someplace there's dirt that I can bring back. Sure, and it ain't the same dirt and I know that. But I know one thing, that old river ain't gonna tear out no more of your land, Amy."

"Our land, Johnny. I ain't got no land without you. No way, I could put no land back by myself. If you was to go find dirt to fill up that wet hole, that'd be your dirt."

"It'd be yours if it was put on your land."

"But not if you put it there. Johnny, you a'fixin' to get thick headed on me again? You been lookin' all over creation for the land with the right dirt. If I didn't have you, that river'd get every scrap and parcel of what Gran left me. It's plain to see that all I got here is a place to put the dirt. Now you got a chance to make that dirt be whatever you want. That makes it our dirt."

Johnny stared silently. The girl leaned against him, shivering. Johnny's arm tightened around her shoulders.

"Johnny?"

"Yeah?"

"You listenin'?"

"Yeah, but it don't hardly seem right to say somethin' is mine when it was left to you."

"Can't you hear, Johnny? What Gran left me is gonna be gone. 'Nother thing, Johnny Scott, if you was to turn this around and it was your Gran left it to you, you'd say to me, 'Amy, look at what we got, soon as I get it built up.' And here we stand, the same two people, 'cept it was my Gran, and you're sayin' you feel funny 'bout it.

"You keep thinkin' two ways, Johnny. We gonna be together and what one of us has, belongs to the other one, be it chocolate cake or chickenpox. Good or bad, we both got us a good thing and we both got a problem to be workin' on." She waited a respectable moment, then demanded, "You see that clear, Johnny?"

"Yeah, I got it now. Just needed to hear you say it, plain like, so as I'd know your true feelin' on it."

Mr. Scott and Mr. Darnell were walking back up the riverbank, talking animatedly, raising their voices over the roar of the river and pointing as they described the work to be done.

Mr. Darnell addressed Johnny, "Your pa and me, we thought to give you a few days work, bein' the off season. I can be lookin' around for rip rap rocks and get started in the morning."

And from Mr. Scott, "If we was to find a body blastin' gum stumps, that'd fill in fast, bein' heavy and not be likely to rise and float away."

Johnny looked at his pa and then at Amy's pa. "Whatever things you want to haul in here, they gonna be appreciated. Seems there'll be places enough for everything." No one looked at Amy, nor did she expect them to. This was man's conversation. She looked at the swirling water and thought of Gran. The green eyes swam with salty tears that broke loose and flowed as the men talked.

She shivered, uncontrollably, and Johnny reached for her hand. "I got'a be takin' Amy in out'a this weather. I'd be obliged for what you gonna do, and thanks."

He hurried to the buggy and the restless Brushy pranced in eagerness to be moving, possibly to the warm, livery stable. A sheepskin lap robe in the buggy hugged warmly around Amy's legs, but her feet were damp from standing on the wet ground in light-soled shoes.

Johnny felt under the robe, seeking her hand. Her fingers were icicles. She caught Johnny's hand and held it tight in both of hers. It felt warm and strong. My Johnny. Gran's gone but I still have you and you're not gonna get away.

Mr. Jenkins' sister met them at the door, enveloping her in a smothering embrace. "Child, we thought and thought about you and your loss. We got the same thing starin' at our faces, come time Ma got'a leave us. Some things just got'a be stood, bein' no way to duck around 'em."

21

MONDAY MORNING FOUND Amy back at the Mercantile. Her hair was piled high and decorated with a fancy blue comb. She wore her favorite blue serge winter church dress with the velvet collar. She was carefully and tastefully attired on the outside, but inside, she was empty. She was surprised to find the store seeming like a comforting friend and she found solace with the buttons and shoes. Many ladies, passing by and seeing her through the plate glass windows, dropped in to offer sympathy and tell of their own similar losses. Amy listened, drawing comfort from their concern. As the ladies chatted, they looked around the store and most of them bought some small item before they left.

This was the day for the salesman with his catalog of shiny pictures to come calling on Mr. Jenkins. The owner and the salesman would sit and talk, or maybe go to the cafe and have a cup of coffee while they discussed the next order. This salesman, a new one for the route, tipped his hat to Amy, "Be your father here today?"

Mr. Jenkins came from the back room in time to hear the question. "That young lady there is not my daughter, though it wouldn't trouble me too much if she was. But she ain't. Been thinkin' that when one of you fellows came around again, she'd be the one you'd need to talk to about what's needed over there." He waved an elbow toward the neatly arranged woman's corner. "Like as not, she'd be better pickin' out what a woman wants than I'd be. 'Sides, that's what I pay her for.... talkin'." He chuckled and wiped his hand across his brow. "Got'a warn you about her talkin', though. That young lady'd be able to talk a flea out'a its hide, any day and twice on Sunday. I got things to do in the back, so I want her to look at the book and see what's to be ordered." Then Mr. Jenkins disappeared.

It would have been difficult to note which was the more surprised, Amy or the salesman. He seemed dismayed at the looming prospect, but handed the catalog to her. Her hand trembled slightly and she felt breathless as she opened the colorful book. Fascinating things would be inside, and could she really decide what Mr. Jenkins should buy? How would she, the girl from Five-Mile-Hill, know what town women would like? Surely he didn't mean for her to actually look at the catalog and choose, even though that was what he said.

The salesman stood restlesly on one foot, then the other. At this rate, he would never get away from here. Besides, he was hungry.

"Young lady, I got me an idea. It bein' satisfactory with Mr. Jenkins, I could be leavin' that with you so as you could take your time and order everything you need. Got me a stop over in Pixley, and I could pick up the book and talk with him on the way back."

Amy's eyes shone. A whole day and an evening with this wonderful book. Suddenly, she remembered, "You got lady's stockings, the thin kind that are smooth and shiny? I'd think they'd be bought, if we had some."

The salesman took a deep breath. How lucky can one man be! "Let me show you where to find them, young lady. See, right over here." The salesman opened the catalog to the stockings, which were across the page from fancy underthings. Amy felt her face begin to flush.

"Thank you, mister," she said softly, retrieving the catalog. It didn't seem fitting, somehow, to look at underthings with a strange man beside you. "I'll be ready with a list when you come back."

22

THE THOMASON'S WERE staying in that evening, so Amy was free to do as she pleased, not having to be concerned with caring for old Grandma Thomason. She was faced with the decision to study spelling or look at the catalog. The catalog won. The speller would still be with her tomorrow after the catalog was gone.

Curled up in the soft, overstuffed chair in her room, she poured over the pictures of unlimited wonders. In addition to feminine finery, there were stoves, dishes, linoleum floor coverings, smooth and shiny. There were fat, feather-filled pillows, sets of knives and drinking glasses with flowers and birds painted on them. Clearly, the catalog contained more wonders than the heart could fathom.

On a sheet of paper, she listed items she thought the River Bend ladies would like to buy. Among these items were the thick, shiny, thread-wrapped garters that were extremely expensive.

The candle burned low and Amy moved her paper closer to the candle to get more light before the flame went out. She read the list aloud, testing the sound of the items. Yes, this is what Mr. Jenkins should order.

The small candle was only a guttering flame as she turned back her quilt to go to bed. That was when she noted the small, embroidered candle Gran had put on her quilt. She remembered Gran's words that the candle was to remind her to check over and inspect the products of her hand, and not to let her candle go out until she had finished her tasks. Her finger traced the outline of the threads and tears filled her eyes. Gathering an armful of the quilt, she buried her face to smother the sobs, and finally exhausted sleep claimed her.

When the alarm sounded, she startled awake, distressed that she had slept in her work dress. She hurriedly changed and looked in the mirror of her dresser. The indentation of a small daisy was imprinted on her cheek where she had lain against Gran's stitches. The yellow daisy. That's what Gran had said she reminded her of. Strong, hardy and with many flowers it grew. If all the flowers were picked, the daisy would hurry and make more flowers. Crying herself to sleep was not the way to be strong with many flowers. No more of that, Miss Amy, she told herself, sternly.

Mr. Jenkins only glanced at her carefully prepared list. What did he know about women's things, anyway? She felt her heart swelling within her, taking her breath away. She had made the decision of what to order, now it was up to her to sell everything and justify her choice.

When the salesman came by, there were even more surprises. "We have a few things we'd like to leave here on our Consignment Plan. You don't have to pay for them unless the young lady sells them. If she hasn't sold them in two weeks. I'll pick them up."

Mr. Jenkins looked at Amy, who nodded, then he told the salesman he might leave the merchandise. The girl stared in wonder as the salesman brought out shiny broaches, fancy combs, handkerchiefs made of delicate lace, also night gowns and robes of shiny material. Amy sighed a long sigh of anticipation. Just wait till the ladies came in and saw these things!

On Sunday afternoon, a week after Amy had first seen her land, Johnny came to pick her up in the buggy. They were going to look at it again, just the two of them. A cutting wind swept down the valley, and Amy huddled gratefully under the sheepskin robe.

Together, they stood beneath the overcast sky, looking at the brown water. Near the willow trees, prints of sled runners and hoofs of the mules scared the brown grass. A few stones were on the bank, showing where the fathers had been at work. Johnny knelt and reached under the icy water. The river bottom was a thick layer of mud, even after the stones had been dumped. Obviously, rip-rapping would be ineffective until the water current was slowed. Amy waited and watched silently, her hands tucked into her coat sleeves for warmth.

Johnny dried his hands on his handkerchief. "Been thinkin'. Workin' all day up there on that mountain, all I see in my mind is the way that river keeps cuttin' away. Time I get back to town, ain't nothin' left of the winter daylight to be doin' somethin' about it. Talked to 'em down at the coal company and they thought, seein' I was hauled ahead, I could have me some time off on condition I'd come on back if they was to get behind. Told 'em I'd be glad of that, bein' I had such a problem.

"Seemed I was workin' for money to get land and now the land don't need the money, much as it needs the time. Nobody needs to be workin' on this here washout 'cept me. Your pa and mine spent time a'bringin' rocks down here just to be ate up by the mud. Got'a think on a way to do it better."

As they stood on the bank, a man approached them, walking down the slope of the hill across the road. He greeted them, "You'd be the youngens who owns this strip? Sure glad to see you lookin' down at that water, the way it needs to be stopped, right away."

Johnny held out his head, "Johnny Scott. This is Amy Catherine Darnell. Her Gran left her this strip when she passed on."

The man nodded at Amy. "Ma'am, proud to see you. Been wantin' to talk to a member of the family on another matter. Up in the grove yonder, they's a cabin made out'a cedar logs. Floor must's been oak, 'cause it's rotted out, but them cedar logs is fair turned to stone. They was well treated when they was put up. Vines and trees are eatin' away at the cabin. Hacked 'em back, a time or two, but they grow so fast they stay up ahead'a me.

"Wish you youngens could see your way clear to come up and give a look. I'd as soon have the building out'a that cedar grove, but couldn't bring myself to burn it down. Could you walk up there now and look at it, so as I'd know?"

"Sure thing, Mr....?"

"McDuff's the name. Marvin McDuff. Bought this land off the old lady that must'a been your grandma. Studied about why she kept that strip, bein' so long and narrow. See now, she had herself a purpose."

By now they were working their way under the cedar limbs of the ancient grove. Wild berry vines and muscadine grapes grew together to weave a hedge about the cabin.

"Found myself doin' a lot'a choppin' away at the grapes and ivy. Figure if you got access to a couple'a strong mules, you could maybe drag some of that thicket down gettin' them logs away. That'd be a help to me and likely you could find a use for them cabin logs."

Johnny stepped over the fallen, rotted door of the cabin. Leaves, twigs and exploring vines had found their way into the interior. Spiders had webbed the rafters and dirt dauber wasps had constructed their clay nurseries in the corners. An old barn swallow nest of hardened clay hung from the loft.

Johnny opened his knife blade and pitched it against the log wall. With a "ping", the knife glanced off the log, falling on the rotted floor. He picked it up and flipped it toward a rafter. The glancing force of the throw closed the knife blade into its sheath, and it fell, again, to the rotting floor.

Mr. McDuff nodded with satisfaction. "Told ya the truth about them logs bein' took care of. Them wide beams nigh turned themselves into stone, bein' that old. Most likely they'll weigh like stone, too, draggin' against a pair'a mules."

Johnny nodded. "Don't have me no mules, but I got a pair of Clydesdales what'll drag down them timbers and not break a sweat."

"You got Clydesdales? Then you'll sure enough want to be movin' this here cabin."

Amy wandered away, unnoticed, as the man-talk went on. Outside the cabin, on a low limb, was a bird nest left from last summer. A thick blanket of dropped needles carpeted the ground, creating a pungent odor of resin and organic decay. Gran had looked at these cedars and liked them. She had walked on this ground and looked at the bird's nests in the trees. Amy looked up into the cedars, her heart aching with sad loneliness.

The men emerged from the cabin door.

"Be comin' 'round to get started on this first thing in the mornin'. Them logs got'a be numbered, first, and I can drag a path wherever you say."

"Sure thing."

Johnny ducked under limbs and came to where Amy stood. The damp air seemed heavier and a light moisture was falling, stinging against their faces. Johnny, however, seemed as happy as if it had been a warm, spring day.

"We got us a bit'a luck," he told her, cheerfully. "Had a thought, over there in that cabin. 'Stead'a usin' them logs to put us up a cabin, I can move this'n, just like it is. Move all them logs and just put it back together like a jigsaw puzzle, almost. That'd give me a place to stay while I was a'workin' on that river. Seems that'd be even better than stayin' at the livery in my wagon."

They walked down the slope and across the road to their own land, "We could think on where to put it. Later it could be your summer kitchen after I put up a bigger house for us. Or we could build onto it. What'd you think'a livin' in your Gran's cabin? Wouldn't be makin' you sad, would it?"

"Sad? Livin' in Gran's cabin? Can't see why it would."

"Wanted to be sure. Them's good logs. Gonna save us a sight'a time."

They walked toward the buggy and the fidgeting Brushy. The drizzle of rain was coming down heavier, now.

"How long you think it'll take to get the cabin up?"

"Don't rightly know, never havin' done it. Figure the better part of a week, anyway."

"Workin' alone?"

"Reckon so. I'm all I got."

"Johnny, you and me, we're gettin' to be strangers. Ain't we ever got no time to talk, you and me?"

"We could get married. Then there'd be time to talk."

"Now, Johnny, don't go to twistin' my words. I got studyin' to do. Bein' alone has made me get more studyin' done. I got'a get that certificate 'afore we get married. I never heard of no woman that was married, passin' a test to teach school."

The streets of River Bend were dark. The light from the oil lamps made yellow squares of brightness, all up and down the street.

"Johnny, we got nigh onto $500.00 we earned and over $200.00 of what Gran left for taxes. We got lots of money and we got no land to buy."

"Yep, seems strange, somehow, don't it? If you was to want to quit workin' at the Merchantile, you could think on it."

But Amy responded, "Be better for us if it was you quittin'. Things that got'a be done are things I can't do."

"Does sound that'a'way. Can't though. Promised 'em I'd take on the winter, givin' 'em all the time they needed. They promised me and I promised them. Got a promise to keep. Need to take what days I can, 'cause we ain't through buyin' yet, and this'n's a good winter job. Maybe for next year, too."

By now they were in front of the Thomason's. The front door of the house opened and the yellow lamplight shone a welcome into the darkness.

"You be out there, Amy, honey? We was fixin' to be worried where you was."

"Yes, it's me. I'm comin'."

It was the next day at the Mercantile that Amy's brother, Dave, came in the store. He stepped carefully over to the woman's corner.

"You bein' all right, Amy? Mama and Louise been after me to stop in and see about you."

She nodded, "Doin' fine, Dave."

Her brother continued, "How's that old Johnny gettin' on? Ain't seen 'im to talk to since back last summer. He keepin' busy and makin' money?"

A frown creased Amy's forehead. "Dave, Johnny's aimin' to take him on somethin' big. The man bought Gran's place gave me the logs in Gran's old cabin. Johnny's set to move it onto our land, log by log, so as he can stay there and work on the wash."

"Good idea. Them's logs that'll last forever and a day, bein' oiled the way they was against the weather and all. Likely turned to stone by now."

"That ain't it, Dave. Johnny's 'bout done in, workin' and a'worryin', and he could use a day's help."

Dave grinned, affably. "Shucks, I could get the boys together and we could give 'im a day. Us five and his team, we should get that cabin up in a day. Easy."

"Oh, Dave, could you?"

"Don't see why not? Been wantin' to see old Johnny, anyway. Tell 'im, day after tomorrow, if he don't hear different, we'll be there."

A lady came in the store and Amy turned to greet her with a smile. "Mornin, there, Miz Markham."

Dave looked around, nervously. "I got'a go, now. You tell Johnny."

"Thank you, Dave. Miz Markham, that wind 'bout freeze the skin off you out there?"

Mr. Jenkins glanced at Amy, repeatedly, and strained his ears but he just couldn't hear what Mrs. Markham was saying to her. He edged closer, but the woman turned her back to him. He was forced to occupy himself with the kegs of tacks and nails, bolts and nuts. Mrs. Markham stayed and talked with Amy for an uncomfortably long period of time. When she finally left without buying something, he was truly concerned.

"Young lady, come over here, will you? See these here kegs of nails and things? I was thinkin' if maybe I moved them to the back room, along with them harnesses, there'd be more room along here for the hats and shoes. Then if there was more things in the book you could see, that maybe women would want, we could put 'em in here without crowdin'."

Amy looked, thoughtfully, down at the kegs. There were seven of them, stretched out in a row. The sides of the kegs were splintery and rough, causing ladies to give them a wide berth as they came down the aisle, for fear of splinters in their clothes.

Mr. Jenkins continued. "I been thinkin' on somethin' else. Figure you to be worth two dollars a day, now, 'stead of a dollar and a half, so that'd be your pay, startin' now."

"I'll be thankin' you, Mr. Jenkins. I got somethin' to ask."

Mr. Jenkins waited, silently, watching her face for signs of restlessness.

She confided, "Miz Markham was talkin' private with me, not wantin' no listenin', in on account of shame. She says she's been wantin' one of them sewin' machines like they make bought dresses on, and she done said to all the ladies that she knows how to work one of 'em. But she don't. Trouble is, she got carried away in her story tellin', her not ever havin' a chance to touch one of them machines."

Amy paused for breath and Mr. Jenkins stared, puzzled, at the girl's anxious face.

She continued, "She was thinkin' maybe I know about 'em. Fact is, I ain't no better. She says to me, if I could get the salesman to show me how to use one of them machines, and if I was to show her in private, like, she'd buy one of them machines from the Mercantile." She smiled, weakly. "They got them machines for sale in the catalog for sixteen dollars."

Mr. Jenkins sighed with relief. If Amy had, at that moment, asked him to give her his most expensive hat, he would gladly have done so. He told her, "No trouble to that. We just got'a have one of them machines dropped by. We'll find a place in the back till you learned about it."

Her face was still a mask of concern, "But, Mr. Jenkins, happen I try to learn to work that machine and I ain't smart enough to learn. Then me and Miz. Markham, both'd look the fool."

Mr. Jenkins studied Amy's face, soberly, then at the corner of his mouth, there came a tiny twitch. Then he could restrain himself no longer and dissolved in laughter. "I swear, young lady, you could talk a Eskimo out'a his ice house, and it snowin'. Worst thing about all this bein' how hard it'll be to keep from blabbin' it, bein' too good of a story to be stayin' in my head. I got me a picture of you teachin' every woman in River Bend how to use that sewin' machine, right here in my back room."

Amy registered her relief with a grin.

Mr. Jenkins continued, "Thing is, I'm thinkin' to offer you a deal. If you was to learn Miz Markham in private, and not tell a soul, then we could set that machine over by the window and you could offer to teach other women. I'm sayin' there'd be an extra dollar for you for every one of them women you sell a machine to. Seen women comin' in, askin' you this and that, there'd be a sight'a yard goods we'd sell."

"But Miz Markham says she wants to buy that machine."

"Child, we gonna have that salesman bring us two. Maybe three or four." With that pronouncement, Mr. Jenkins began to work the first of the nail kegs across the rough floor to the back room.

Amy had her own thoughts. If sixteen women came in to buy a machine from her, that would be sixteen dollars, enough to buy one for herself.

Johnny's relief was profound when he saw his five friends waiting on site, their wagons lining the road. One of the wagons contained a sizeable heap of hand-shaped wooden shingles.

The oldest of the brothers explained, "Had me a heap'a shingles left over from the ones me and Pa axed out when I was puttin' up a shed. Had no plans for 'em for goodness knows when, so I pitched 'em in the wagon. Figured you'd find a use for 'em."

Mr. McDuff was also relieved to see the help. "Bein' so many of you young men, there'd be no need for me to stay here and be in the way. I'll just build up a fire for you to warm up to, time to time." The old man stared up, apprehensively, at the high blown cirrus clouds, known to be the bringers of snow. "Gonna have us snow by Christmas, I'd wager."

Johnny also looked up, dutifully. "Could be, Mr. McDuff. But it don't need to do no snowin' just for me. I reckon I could struggle along without it."

With the help of the log chains, the cabin walls were pulled over. The Clydesdales leaned into the traces and the settled logs of fifty years ago now lay in jack-straw piles in the cedar grove.

The massive coal wagon was drawn up as close as possible, for the logs were to be loaded by hand. At Johnny's urging, the powerful animals pulled the loaded wagon down the slope, across the road and onto the site selected by Johnny and Amy. The first load brought logs from the lower part of the cabin. The second load brought two of the brothers who began to reassemble the cabin according to the numbers Johnny had painted on the logs.

Dave commented, "J.T., lookie there at them log joints. Looks like our old granddad swung hisself a good ax, by the fit of 'em. Don't hardly need no clay packin'."

"Yep, and note how they was oiled 'afore they was put together. Ain't no rot, nowhere. No bugs nor beatles. Reckon them logs'd last till the judgment day. Maybe longer."

The old shingles were pitched into a pile and Mr. McDuff sorted through them, saving the usable ones and feeding the broken splinters to the fire. By mid morning, all the logs were at the new site and he allowed the fire to die away. He climbed up the hill to his own warm house, pausing first, to see in the distance, the waist high walls of the reconstructed cabin. Youthful strength was a wonderful thing!

By late afternoon, the rafters were up and by nightfall, the tired builders were tapping the shingle base into place. "Shame we couldn't'a got them shingles nailed on 'afore dark. Happen we weren't slowed up by the cold on our hands, it'd'a been a easy trick to be through by now."

But Johnny assured them, "Don't you be thinkin' on that. With what you fellows done, finishin' up gonna be a pure pleasure to me. Got lots'a time, now."

"T'ain't nothing. Consider it a weddin' present. When's it gonna be?"

"Amy thinks maybe spring or early summer. She's got that studin' to do and I got that old river to fight."

"Johnny," Willie began, then hesitated to criticize. "You think you might look where our pa's put them rocks? Quit too soon, they did, and the current's whippin' out the eddy back of 'em. Wisht they hadn't put 'em in there if that was all they had time to haul. Should'a left 'em on the bank."

Johnny agreed. "I know, Willie. Reckon they got busy at home. I got'a get out there and do some levelin'. They'd be enough to hold agin the wash, if it was summer, but I got that run-off from the War Eagle still a'gougin' it out. Reckon they thought they'd get it leveled 'afore the storm came in. I'm grateful for what they brought, anyway."

The brothers went away in their separate wagons, their tired mules plodding toward the mountains and their warm stalls with sweet hay.

Early on Wednesday morning, Brushy was again headed back to the cabin against his will. No moisture was falling, but all surfaces were covered with frost and ice crystals. Brushy was left on the downwind side of the cabin as Johnny gathered an armload of the shingles. Bringing the can of nails, he climbed to the roof. Moisture had frozen the nails into a clump in the bottom of the can. A whack of the hammer cracked them loose and Johnny began to nail shingles to the roof. As he prepared to go to the ground for more shingles, he saw the spot of red on the new wood he had just tapped in place. He touched the red, puzzled, and it felt smooth and hard under his finger. Then he saw the back of his hand, oozing blood along a crimson line. He hadn't even felt it when a jagged shingle edge tore the skin.

The weary young man just shrugged at the blood and continued down the ladder. Taking Brushy's bridle, the pony following, stiff legged, Johnny led him into the protection of the walls and the partially shingled roof. Ice crystals were again falling, slashing at Johnny's face and bare hands as he climbed the ladder with another armload of shingles.

The job that should have taken two hours was finished more than five hours later, and Johnny wasted another fifteen minutes staring at the rising water of the Tuscalara River. Sticks, leaves and trash had plastered themselves against the stonewall of the land spit. The current slapped water against the riverbank, clawing at the soil. Water still oozed gently through the riprap stones and finally Johnny turned wearily and walked away.

It was a full eighth of a mile before the pony regained full use of his stiff legs, then he galloped dead ahead, through the reins were only looped over the saddle horn. Johnny had pushed his frozen hands under his coat and held them against his warm, wool shirt to thaw out his fingers.

At the stable, he felt stinging needles in his feet and ankles as he stepped to the sawdust covered floor. Each step produced shooting pains up his calves. He simply could not face the prospect of sleep on the hay in the icy stable. He needed warmth. And the sight of his girl.

He left the livery stable, noting the still lighted cafe, and walked rapidly to the Thomason's house. Mr. Thomason admitted him at the door and called to Amy. "Why, Johnny, I wouldn't'a thought of you bravin' the mountain on a night like this, just to come and see this here girl. Gonna be rough goin', come time you start headin' home."

His wife added, "If you think that boy gonna climb that mountain in this storm, you got one more think a'comin'." Johnny looked from one to the other and stammered, "I was just a'gonna take her over to the cafe for a cup'a chocolate, and maybe warm up a little."

Mrs. Thomason smiled, knowingly. "You do that, son, then come back her and spend the night in our back room. I got bedrooms I don't even look into from one week to the next. Fact is, if you think your folks won't worry, it'd be a pleasure to put you up till after this storm blows over."

At that point, Amy came into the room carrying her coat.

"Amy, honey, first you go into the pantry and make this boy a couple'a sandwiches out'a that ham from supper. Must'a come down three, maybe four, miles out'a them mountains, gonna make him hungry. Then he can take you out for chocolate."

So Johnny spent a wonderful night on a feather tick under a goose-down comforter and dreamed of ambling on a dusty summer road in a buggy with his girl beside him. He was thinking of how warm the sun felt.

After Johnny had gone to bed in the spare bedroom, Mrs. Thomason looked up from her knitting and said to her husband. "Gonna rest easier, now. Been worryin' the life out'a me, that boy stayin' over at the livery these cold nights, eatin' goodness knows what, and no woman to do for 'im. Been askin' the Good Lord to help me get that boy over here out'a the cold, and now He done it. Gonna be a trick, figurin' how to hold 'im here till he gets that cabin in the dry so's he can have some heat."

Mr. Thomason smiled to himself behind the newspaper. Johnny may as well settle in comfortably because between Mrs. Thomason and the Good Lord, there was no chance he would get away.

Come morning, even the Clydesdales were reluctant to leave their shelter. The sleet had stopped but the low hanging clouds seethed with blackness and high wind. Every tree was stripped of leaves except the blackjack oaks, whose thick, papery leaves rustled, dryly.

Johnny left the lumberyard with the oak door and the plate glass windows he had ordered, also the stovepipe and a potbellied iron stove. He left the Mercantile with a large kettle, a box of salt and 20 pounds of beans.

At the cabin site, he tied the horses to the downwind side of the cabin, but even there, the wind tore at them causing their eyes to water. Finally, in sympathy, he urged their large bodies through the cabin doorway. Their size would help heat the cabin once he got the windows in. He needn't have stopped for the beans because it was late afternoon before he got the pipe sections in place and the stove bolted together. He brought in several armloads of old shingles to dry out, and guided the horses back through the door to hitch them to the wagon.

Then he walked down to the river's edge. As he watched, a mat of grass, leaves and sticks floated against the clay bank. More trash had built up behind the rock spit, stopping some of the flow of water through the riprap stones.

He told Amy that evening, "Happen we don't get no more rain, some kind'a dam could be built up behind them rocks."

And she told him, "Johnny Scott, don't you be wastin' your time and breath sayin' that. One eyeful of them clouds hangin' on the mountaintops tells you water gonna come down out'a there, what'll make Noah's little old flood look like a puddle, it comin' down so fast. Best to think on what to do with the crater that'll be dug out'a the bank when it's gone."

Johnny signed, wearily, "Reckon you're right. Just didn't want'a think on it that a'way."

Johnny ate thick pork chops with fried potatoes, gravy, biscuits and canned peaches with the family, thinking of what could be used to fill up a hole twenty to twenty five feet deep.

The rain came. The first water wall passed through Jacksonville at eleven o'clock, heading for River Bend. The second and larger wall followed three hours later.

At five in the morning, the water swirled against the bank and flowed gently, determinedly, over the newly placed rocks. The second wall pounded against the dam, falling heavily over the far side. The weight of the falling water dug at the riverbed, causing the stones to fall into the gouged out spot. The force of the scouring water loosened clods of soil that had not been touched since the earth's creation.

Each inch gouged from the bottom of the pool made just that much farther for succeeding waves of water to fall, causing even more soil to be torn and dug away at an even faster pace. Rich, black dirt blended with the clay particles thickening the Tuscalara river. In the darkness of the back room bed, Johnny could see the happenings as clearly as though he stood on the bank. He twisted and turned under the warm comforter.

The next day, he took a log chain to the cabin. After the potbelly stove was stoked and the beans put in the kettle, he headed for the water with an ax in his hand.

A large willow tree came down first, then a full-branched cedar at least 30 feet high followed the willow. The horses dragged the downed trees to the sunken rocks. With a stout rope, Johnny made a hard knot around a strong old willow growing on the bank and the other end he tied around his waist. Couldn't afford to be swept downstream. Removing his shoes, he walked carefully, stealthily, into the knee-deep, rushing water. In the first seconds, his feet were numb and in minutes he was trembling from the cold. Reaching into the water, he tore at the grass matting and, bending even lower, with the icy water reaching his shoulders, he worked loose the top layer of rocks from one small section. This caused the water to concentrate its current at one spot. Then he forced his numb feet to take him to the bank.

He pushed the willow tree into the water above the dam, working it to the gap in the wall that he had just created. He must attempt to block the trash from falling through. He tied the stout rope to the base of the cedar and looped it around the standing willow, then attached it to the horses. They easily levered the cedar into the hole, settling the base of it into the deepest part.

The noise of the gushing waterfall was immediately quieted as its rush of water coursed through the dense limbs of the cedar, and it broke the force of its fall. With a section of the rope, he lashed the base of the cedar to the standing willow, also.

Johnny had no feeling lower than his hips as he forced his feet to take him to the cabin. The stove was warm and the beans were bubbling but it took Johnny the rest of the day to feel any warmth in himself. When the beans had bubbled tender, Johnny realized a bowl and a spoon would have been convenient but that was only a small problem. With his knife and a piece of shingle, he shaped a spoon and ate beans directly from the pot.

He brought his quilts from the livery and carried them to the warm sleeping loft. Before darkness fell, he was asleep to the sounds of the raging water and the snort and footsteps of the Clydesdales who occupied the cabin with him. The storm passed over in the night and rays of morning sun aroused Johnny from his exhausted sleep.

The road to the coal seam was not yet passable, so Johnny walked to the river to assess his handiwork of yesterday. The river was down, somewhat, and the flow was diffused as it passed through the limbs of the cedar. At first glance, it seemed the tree had settled into the mud but closer inspection revealed that the mud and debris had settled out from the water around its limbs. That took care of the riprap hole, temporarily. Now for the bank.

The small willows had to be the answer. If he cut them and tied them in tight bundles at the bank, the water would be caused to slow down and consequently drop its load of silt without picking up any more.

Willows, growing the length of the river, were readily available. If they still had their summer leaves, that would have been better, but their fine network of limbs would still work. The day was young and Johnny was rested. How much could be done, today?

After a breakfast of cold beans, he hitched the Clydesdales to a length of chain and picked up his ax. The trees on the bank would be first. They were easily spared as willows replace themselves in two or three years, if the roots are left.

The first trees were placed so their tops extended into the water. At first, they swayed with the current, but then plastered themselves against the bank in a solid mass. It was now noon.

Johnny fed the horses and ate a lunch of beans, then he walked up to Mr. McDuff's house. "Happen you got willow trees you want to get out'a the way, I'd make use of 'em."

Mr. McDuff stroked his chin and considered the question. "I got willows and you're welcome. Could you make use of cedar limbs? This whole stand needs trimmin'. Got four big trees need takin' all the way out. You wantin' to go that far?"

"Sure thing, Mr. McDuff. I'll get them four cedars out and the rest of 'em trimmed."

Four massive cedars fell before Johnny's ax. He severed the limbs and chopped out the tops, lashing them together in huge, fragrant bunches, their resiny twigs slashing him across the face in stinging swipes. The cedar trunks he left until later.

At the river, the cedar limbs were tied in bunches and worked in with the willows. When he stepped off the day's work, two hundred feet of bank had been protected and more than twice that was left to go. The cold winter sun was setting over the western range of mountains but if Johnny had not run out of rope, he would have dragged down another bunch of limbs.

Work fully absorbed him and he had not seen Amy for three days.

She saw him pass the Mercantile, but he did not return after stabling the horses. She waited and watched and later, in her room, tears soaked the satiny stitches of Gran's embroidery. Don't be such a baby, she told herself, but salty rivers rained down on the picture of a tree with a swing on one limb. She was tired and lonely. It had been work by day and study by night, and each period of time seemed endless.

Johnny took more rope, crackers and cheese back to the cabin. The horses needed rest to be able to haul coal, but one trip more for branches would not be too much for them. Tying the clusters of limbs together, he dragged the hundred foot long string of cedar brush down the hill.

The next evening, Amy forced herself to study. She read until her eyes burned and then she threw herself across her bed and cried her tears on the pile of hickory nuts and chestnuts her Gran had put on the quilt to remind her of good times. "Oh, Gran, this ain't the way things was gonna be. What am I doin' wrong? How come you left me? I need you, Gran!" But Gran was not there and finally she slept.

On Sunday, she sat with old Grandma Thomason and studied. She read aloud to give the old lady something to think about. She had finished the English and spelling, now, and she would review them later. On to the History

Finally Johnny came. Amy stared in horror at his face. "Johnny, you comin' down with the measles? You hadn't ought'a be out in this wind and sun. You aimin' to kill yourself?"

Johnny grinned at her concern. "Ain't measles. Just got poked and slashed by them cedar limbs I put in the river. When the folks get here to stay with Grandma Thomason, I'll show you what I done."

Later, the buggy jogged along the frozen ruts of the road as the jubilant Brushy, free of the stable at last, was allowed to run. The two miles seemed but a short distance.

"The cabin! Oh, don't it look purty, settin' there next to the river. New shingles? You didn't make 'em, did you? 'Course you didn't! You didn't have no time. I see smoke. You got a fire in there? You got a stove?"

Johnny let her talk, enjoying the sight of her and the sound of her voice. He loved the sparkle of her green eyes and the deepness of her dimple. He had a lifetime to answer her questions. Her chatter continued.

"We got'a think where we want to put my fruit seedlin' trees. And we got'a get a barn and a well. Johnny, what's that green stuff along side'a the river?"

Johnny directed Brushy to take them to the water's edge. "That's what I done with the cedar branches."

Amy stared in fascination. "Tied together just like Christmas trimmin'. You think that'll stop the water? Johnny, where is the place we was worried about?"

"See for yourself," Johnny invited as they moved along.

"You got a whole tree in that water! Johnny, you been out in there gettin' yourself wet! It's a wonder you ain't down sick."

Brushy drew up in front of the cabin. "Oh, lookie, a store bought door! It's beautiful!" She stepped over the threshold. "Johnny, horses been in here! You been bringin' them Clydesdales in here, haven't you?"

"Had no choice. Horses been use to bein' in at night ain't safe to leave 'em out in a storm. Can't be havin' us no sick horses. Got us a stove and it's done been cooked on," he bragged.

"Johnny, you been stayin' out here?"

"Sure I been stayin' out here. Where else would a fellow stay when he's got hisself a new cabin? Got'a have a shed for them horses, though, and I don't know where I'll be gettin' the poles."

"You right about gettin' them horses out'a here." she agreed, stepping over a semi-fresh deposit left on the dirt floor by the animals.

Johnny ignored her. "I figured out why folks wait till spring to relocate. Too much stuff got'a be done in the fall to get ready for winter. Firewood, hay for the livestock, sheds for bad weather. All them things that got'a be done are eatin' at me while the river keeps on eatin' at the bank. Everything got'a come 'afore the next thing, and me out here like a feather in a twister, a'tryin' to get at it."

The excited girl looked around her. The plate glass windows were shiny clean and the logs fitted tight together but had not been chinked. Chill fingered winds forced their way inside.

"Didn't chink them logs yet, Amy. Couldn't. That clay been froze like'a rock."

"You're only one person, Johnny Scott, even while you're tryin' to be six or seven."

Johnny wasn't listening. "Thinkin' about usin' cement 'stead'a clay. Last longer and looks purty and white."

"Then let's do it. We got money."

"Yeah, my head says that, but the poor man inside me keeps on thinkin' poor."

"Got somethin' for you to look at. Salesman left a catalog. We got'a pick out things to buy."

"What things?"

Amy whirled around. "Look around you, Johnny. We need everything."

Johnny was digesting that fact and she continued, "'Nuther thing, we got'a wait till April to get married. I got'a take that test first and I ain't gonna be ready till then."

Johnny reached for her hand. "Three months and a week is a lot'a time waitin'."

"But we got'a."

"Don't know why. You ain't gonna need that paper, married to me, do you think?"

"Likely not, but it's somethin' I got'a do. Puts me in the mind'a you wantin' bottom land. Like an itch that don't get scratched till you get what you want."

Put that way, Johnny understood. Certain things had no reason back of them, they just were. They didn't come and they didn't go, they were just a part of everything

"We ain't got no light," she observed.

"Ain't needed one yet."

"Johnny, I got'a go back."

"Nope. Been too long, you bein' in town and me out here. You ain't goin', just yet."

"I got'a."

"Then we got'a go out and talk about them fruit trees. I was thinkin' they'd be purty in one long row from one end of the land to t'other. Think that'd be too strung out?"

She looked from one direction to the other. "No reason not. Be purty in the spring, all of 'em in bloom."

"Have to fence 'em in. Don't know how I'm gonna get them rails cut along with haulin' coal and fightin' the river."

"Johnny, you ever think'a buyin' rails? And maybe cordwood for the stove? We got money. Buyin' them things'd be like buyin' time off'a some fellow that's got more time than money."

"Hmmmm, well....." It was a thought.

Bundled in the sheepskin robe, they headed back to town.

Christmas was to be spent with the families, the morning at Johnny's house and the afternoon, when the brothers came, would be spent with Amy's parents.

Johnny's pa explained, "Son, it's been a worry to me, not gettin' down there to help at the riverside. Things just kind'a piled up and the storm came in and all, but...."

Johnny nodded, knowingly, "T'ain't the river bein' the biggest bother to me, now, bein' I got past the worst of it with your help. The thing I need most'd be fence rails. Got cows comin' I got'a keep off the road and out'a Amy's fruit trees. Gonna need more'n a mile of railin'. You might put me in the mind of someone with rails to sell."

His pa's eyes brightened. "No, son, you ain't wantin' to spend your money on fence rails, and me with timber needin' to be thinned and a good, sharp ax. Fact is, that'd be a sight easier on me than that rock haulin', bein' close here. I could use spare minutes and get you a lot' rails. Took so much time on Five-Mile-Hill, goin' and comin', hardly got nothin' done down there till it was time to get back here and do the chores. No, son, you ain't wantin' to spend your money on rails."

After Christmas dinner, they went to Amy's house. She was hugged by everyone and she passed out gift boxes of store-bought candles. Mama had made pillowcases, embroidered with flowers and she had made a "Sunday" tea towel. The brother's wives had also embroidered tea towels for her. They were marked "Monday" through "Friday". Her mother explained, "You'll get the "Saturday" towel later.

Johnny's mama wanted to make it and she'd done used up her time on your rug."

Johnny was grateful for the livestock care. "Quick as I get me a day off, some of them animals gonna go to the auction. Must be a sight'a trouble to you."

Amy's pa shook his head. "No, son, you just leave them cows be. Havin' cows is like havin' money walkin' around. One don't hardly have too many. Been usin' the extra milk from 'em to feed out a litter'a pigs. You ought'a see 'em, round and slick as persimmons. Yessiirree, them oinkin' little mortgage lifters gonna bring a good price, and when you get your place, a couple'a gonna be for you and Amy."

He continued, "Keep feelin' bad about not gettin' no more done on that river bank. Seemed like everyday there was some new thing to keep me from gettin' down there. Reckon in a week or two....."

But Johnny interrupted. "No need to worry about that river no more. After you and Pa helped, I got some more done and had a lot'a ideas. I can handle it, now. What I really got'a have now is some fence rails."

"Say no more, son. Splittin' rails is easier than haulin' rocks, any day. Reckon I could hit the timber now and again and get a pile cut up. Couple of months should be enough and then me and your pa could give you a day and string 'em out. Could do that, easy."

"Sure would be a help."

The large family was together, sixteen adults and several small children, gathering in various rooms, exchanging gossip, playing with babies. Christmas night was long and enjoyable. At first light, Johnny came, he and Amy were headed down Five-Mile-Hill, to their jobs.

"That rag rug your mama gave us must'a took a sight'a her time to make. And that other one she promised. Need to get that floorin' down so we can use it. You know, Gran lived for the first year with a dirt floor? Just had sawdust and pine needles coverin' it. Like to'a froze to death, she said. Reckon we gonna have to get the horse pies out'a the other room, first thing."

Johnny did not smile. "Busy as I am, don't know when it'd be."

Amy was not listening. Her hand caressed the embroidered stitches of her gifts, each one a gift of time, stolen from a busy day. These were moments of their life that they lovingly gave to her. The love in the gifts made thrill bumps play up and down her arms. Beside these gifts, the boxed store-bought candles seemed inadequate. Next year she would do better.

She spent the Friday after Christmas at the Mercantile and the evening with her English Composition book. Johnny hauled coal until evening and wrestled the stove back into its place, being careful not to mar the finish of the new floor he had just put down. Tomorrow, he would pick up some nice, dry sticks for a Sunday fire.

On Saturday, Amy awoke to a bustle of activity in the house. Old Grandma Thomason had taken a turn for the worse.

"Holiday's do that to old folks, sometimes," consoled the doctor. As the day wore on, she did not rally and before evening, she was gone. Amy found many things to do as neighbors and towns people stopped by, bringing sympathy and covered dishes of food. Relatives living close enough were there, creating a house seething with people.

Johnny stopped by to pay his respects and left, going home to an empty cabin and no chance to surprise Amy with the new floor. This was truly one occasion, however, when he was glad he was a man and not expected to be an active part of another family's sadness. He found things to do, though, after the church services. He walked from one end of the strip of land to the other, planning. Melons would be planted here by the river. This black dirt might grow corn stalks 12 feet tall. A cross fence would be needed to keep the livestock in place. He probably had too many cows. Maybe he would sell some cows and get a start of those fancy sheep that grew the long wooly hair. Needed a barn, really bad. Had to figure out something soon. And there was the river.

The Mercantile was closed Monday and Tuesday until after the funeral. Wednesday found Amy back at work and that evening she told the family. "Be gettin' my things together and gettin' out, come Sunday when Johnny comes to take me home."

But the lady of the house would not permit it. "You'll do no such of a thing. It ain't no doin' of yours that she's gone on, and you never was no trouble, only a help. Beddin' and food we got lots of and we ain't hearin' no more of that talk. Till you and that young man get married, you're stayin' right here."

So she stayed.

New Year's Day was Thursday and the store was closed. When Johnny came for her, she climbed into the buggy with her catalog, a shiny, new coffee pot and a basket containing sliced turkey, fresh lightbread, plum jelly and a fruitcake in a round, bright colored tin can. "Cake likely won't taste as good as our mama's can make, but I wanted me that can for buttons and things. We got dry wood, Johnny?"

"Enough. Picked up some sticks on the way."

A friendly, cozy thread of smoke lifted from the cabin stovepipe. Brushy pulled the buggy close to the front door, and she jumped out. She opened the fancy door and stepped inside, gasping, "Why, Johnny, they's a floor in this cabin!"

"Reckon how that happened," he responded, with a grin. "Must'a growed there in the night."

"Johnny, you're mean! You could'a told me about that floor and not had me squealin' like a scared chicken." She cast aside her bundles and sat on the floor, smoothing her hand across the glossy oak boards.

"This here's the prettiest floor I ever saw. Look at me, splashin' tears all over our new floor. We got'a get us a mop. Oh, Johnny! What would Gran say if she could see this?"

The oak plank flooring had been expensive and so had the two gallons of shellac to cover it, but, watching his Amy, Johnny felt he had easily gotten his money's worth.

"Johnny, if we'd put this stuff on the walls it'd make them shiny, too, don't you think?"

"Sort'a figured to do that."

The fire crackled and the new rug was soft for sitting. The catalog was thick with colored pictures. The girl spread out a sheet of paper and wrote. They'd need dishes, two kerosene lamps, wall hooks, a pressure canner, a coffee grinder, a butter mold, a candle maker, spoons, forks and knives. The list grew alarmingly.

They picked out a bed with iron scrollwork at the head and foot, a dresser with a big mirror, and a chest. "Ain't this fun?"

They picked out a table and two chairs. "I'll make benches, later."

They ate fruitcake. The sun began to set and Amy lighted one of the colored candles, setting it on a block of wood on the windowsill. The soft glow flickered against the old logs and the shiny floor. It flickered against Amy's green eyes like sparks of fire. It made gold of the sunburned ends of her hair and glowed rosy on her skin. Johnny lay back on the soft rug, so he could better admire her as she read her history book. The quiet and the soft light became more than his weariness could withstand, and his eyes closed with exhaustion. She moved closer to the light, then realized Johnny was sound asleep.

"Johnny, wake up. You got'a take me home."

Brushy knew the routine without direction. He took them to the Thomason's house to let Amy out, then circled and took Johnny home to the cabin, which forced him to spend the night out under the shelter of the porch roof.

23

BY FEBRUARY, THE days had begun to be a bit longer, giving Johnny enough daylight to do a few things. He started the zigzag pattern of the rail fence, making use of the poles that had been cut for him. He followed the road, noting where the fruit trees would be.

He brought home wagon loads of dusty coal slack, knowing how grass loves to grow in the black crumbles and coarse grains of broken coal. It would make a firm driveway, keeping wagon wheels from getting stuck in the soft black dirt come wet weather.

And he worked on the river. Little by little, the silt and clay particles were settling into his tree-lined dam. Later, he knew, he would need other material. In summer, when the current was not so strong, he could add gravel, sawdust from the mills, tree stumps and some heavily rooted vines such as trumpet and honeysuckle. The river was strong, but he would win. All of the land that the river had stolen, he would force it to give back.

New sounds from across the river attracted his attention, and he watched as a double team of Clydesdale pulling a long wagon and bringing a load of long poles, peeled of bark and heavily oiled. The trailer crossed the wagon bridge, off-loading the poles near the concrete abutment across the river. Well, the railroad people were back at work, bringing material for the trestle bridge. He couldn't see extremely well, but they seemed to be piling the poles dangerously near the riverbank.

By the end of February, Johnny had built a temporary lean-to on the house for Brushy, keeping him warmer than the porch overhang, but the Clydesdales were still at the livery. He was careful with his investment animals.

The first of March brought on the rains again. The height of the river rose several inches over night, swirling around the base of the abutment across the river and the new pile of poles. It eased away all the small stones and grass clumps supporting them.

A dead log came rapidly down stream and whirled against the concrete, glanced away and plunged, end first, into the pile of poles. In one movement, the pile shifted, sliding the top pole into the water. At split second intervals, the rest followed, bucking, plunging and rolling down river toward Johnny's handiwork.

The first log plowed into the bank, burying one end in the mud and rearing the other end into the air. The next log knocked the first one against the spillway Johnny had created in the rock spit. The third and all succeeding logs rammed into the new mud and stuck firmly. Thirty-eight poles were slanted into the river, collecting limbs and other debris behind them. If the log jam broke, all of Johnny's work as well as his row of willow trees would no doubt be washed out and on their way to the Mississippi River.

Two days later, the logs were still there, collecting debris. Johnny shook his head in dismay, assessing the damage to be caused by winching the poles out of the mud. The river was still rising.

Hauling coal would be impossible due to the rain, so Johnny took Brushy to town and brought back the Clydesdales. He tossed a lasso toward the first log of the group and followed the rope line into the river, carrying a log chain. He made a secure hook and swam back through the muddy, ice cold water. The horses easily pulled the log from the mud and slid it onto the riverbank. By midnight, twenty-three logs lay side by side on the rushing water.

The rain poured down the next day and Johnny winched ashore fifteen more logs. They measured an exact 30 feet long.

By noon of the third day, working in a cold, driving rain, Johnny had marked out the perimeter of his barn. By dark, it had three walls, high as his head, with six poles left for the ridge. Limp from exhaustion, Johnny and the Clydesdales quit for the day. Early the fourth morning, he went to the lumber yard for a load of decking lumber and shingles, a few nails and some tar for sealing out the leaks.

Three days after that, the rain stopped and he knew the roads to the mountain would soon again be safe to use. Time was short. Johnny hung a lantern on the end of his ladder and hammered shingles all night. Mid morning the next day, he was just finishing when a representative of the railroad came in his yard.

"Those poles you're using, they belong to the railroad and you have to give them back, immediately."

Johnny stood on the ridgepole of his barn with his hammer in his hand and said nothing.

"You hear me? You stole those logs. We want 'em back."

"Didn't steal no logs. Fished these here out'a my mud bank, like I been fishin' out trash all winter. Look at them muddy ends if you don't believe me. But there one thing I know. That railroad of yours took away more'n three acres of my land and I can prove it with a survey. To my thinkin', turn about's fair play. Happen you think that railroad gonna give me back my three acres, I'll think on givin' you my pole barn."

The railroad representative came closer to the foot of the ladder. Johnny continued, "Till you think up a way to bring back my land, I'm hopin' you don't walk up too close to my horse barn. I'm dead-tired and a little shaky and here I stand with a hammer in my hand. Could be I didn't put this barn up too good and these here logs are mighty heavy. Happen they get to rollin', be a sight of the damage they'd do. Just like when they hit my dam. Better step back on that road, mister, just to be safe."

The railroad man backed away and returned to the road, and Johnny tapped the last few shingles into place.

Amy's catalog order came, and suddenly the cabin looked like a home. The shiny new Singer sewing machine took up the space by the best window. Bright new colors of yard goods were spread on the floor and pinned onto the paper patterns. The dresses were basted by hand as she studied English Composition, then sewed on the machine on weekends. Several stylish dresses took shape.

"Gonna make sure I learn good, so when I sew my wedding dress, I'll be all practiced up."

The fashionable new patterns were the very latest styles, puffs in front and ruffles behind. She made gathered and pleated dresses and she made pencil slim dresses with tulip-flared skirts and wore them to work. It was now past the middle of March.

Johnny brought down his livestock as fast as he had fences to contain them. Early vegetables, such as peas, onions and greens were sprouting in his garden.

The felled cedars and willows had sunk below the water and thick clumps of marsh grasses were growing within six and eight feet from the bank, rooted in the dirt caught by the limbs of the dead trees. The four trimmed cedar logs still lay on Mr. McDuff's slope, a constant nag to Johnny's mind.

When the rains again dissolved the mountain road, he took the coal wagon to the cedar grove and winched the logs aboard, their weight burying the wagon wheels more than once, but the powerful horses managed to pull them free. He turned the horses toward Jacksonville and settled in for the wet, lonely ride. Three hours later, he brought them to a halt at the Jacksonville Custom Lumber Company.

"Need to get these logs sawed up, inch and half thick, planed smooth and I want to keep all the scrappy pieces."

They told him, sure thing, and he could get them in a week or so.

Johnny sighed and smiled amiably. "If you can't get to them no sooner, couldn't ask for more. Could you tell me the best place on your lot to park my rig, so as I can wait? Some place out back, maybe, so as I'd not be a bother?"

"Wait, you said what…?"

"Sure thing. No way I can go home without them boards. Makin' a present for my girl's birthday. Somethin' happens I don't get it made, I'd be obliged to look for me another girl and that'd take a sight longer than a week. Reckon I'll just pull in someplace back here and wait."

There was a small conference, and a few furtive glances in the direction of Johnny, the Clydesdales and the huge coal wagon, which was using up most of their parking space. In an hour and forty minutes, the logs were cut and planed and Johnny was headed east, the boards tucked protectively under oilskin tarps.

Daylight was fading as he turned the team into his driveway and bestowed the boards to the recesses of the barn. Making Amy's cedar quilt chest would take another day, maybe two, of his precious time. This gift might be a surprise, but it was no guessing game. There was one thing he was certain of, every girl wanted a cedar chest to store her quilts. Amy would be seventeen in two weeks.

That evening, Johnny persuaded her to come out to the cabin for a while. "Be as easy to study that book one place as another, seems to me."

Johnny lay on the bed to watch her as she studied, frowns of concentration creasing her forehead. Then, in his exhaustion, his weary eyes closed. She glanced at him once, and decided to let him sleep. She sat on the floor, leaning against the bed. The dimness of the light blurred her eyes and she lay her head back to rest them a moment. In an instant, sleep claimed her.

A snort from Brushy startled her awake and she glanced toward Johnny, still sound asleep. Quietly, she slipped on her coat and tied her scarf. She picked up her papers and book, and looked back once more. She put down the book and picked up Gran's thick quilt and spread it over Johnny. Closing the door softly, she climbed into the buggy.

"Let's go, Brushy," she told the impatient pony and he trotted rapidly toward the livery. She had to wake the liveryman to take care of Brushy and the buggy, and he stared at her with sleepy, accusing eyes.

Amy glared at him in the darkness. "What I did was some studyin' in my book here. Takes a sight'a readin' to pass them tests with good marks." With that, she marched out into the darkness.

At the Thomason's, a lamp burned in the window and she let herself in with her key. In the darkness she bumped into a cushiony, rounded figure.

"That you, Amy, honey? I was on the way to the kitchen to get a bit'a milk and maybe make me sleepy."

"It's me. Hope you wasn't kept awake."

"Wasn't that, really. Though we did think you might be havin' a bit'a trouble, somewhere, maybe needin' help. Things ain't like they use to be and there's still some danger to a girl, alone. Honey, you come walkin' in by yourself? Ain't meanin' to be nosey, but your mama or Gran not bein' here, thought maybe I ought'a ask if maybe Johnny...."

"Ain't no problem."

"You mean...?"

"Truth is, I was readin' my book here, and Johnny dropped off to sleep, bein' tired from all he's been doin'. Could'a woke him, but I can drive that buggy well as he can, so I thought to let him sleep."

The soft arms enveloped her. "Child, your words are a relief to me, worryin' the way I did, and I'll not deny it. What you done was what I'd'a done, myself. Goodnight, now."

"Goodnight."

Morning saw Johnny at the Thomason's door, bright and early. "Amy, you oughtn't'a done that, drivin' down that road all alone, at night."

"Bein' alone was better'n havin' somethin' else in there with me, you bein' asleep in the cabin," she retorted, impudently.

"You know what I mean. Should'a woke me."

"And you deader'n a doornail? Likely the burnin' down'a the cabin wouldn't'a woke you."

So Johnny left to drive his team up the mountain to the coal seam.

Amy looked at wedding dresses in the catalog. They looked like something an angel would wear..... heavy, shiny satin and light filmy tulle. The price was forty-three dollars. There were dresses in colors for the bride's best friend. That would be Louise, her brother Dave's wife. The price of the yellow dress she liked was twenty-two dollars.

She thumbed through the catalog searching for the yard goods. Ah, there it was! She could get slipper satin, tulle, ribbons and lace. Buttons and braid and fancy beads. She'd need eight yards of white satin and a lot of trimming. Yellow taffeta for Louise, made up so it would be a good Sunday dress for the rest of the summer.

Customers came and she put away the catalog to greet them with a smile. She had a job to do and even the plans for her wedding would have to be put aside.

Johnny knew the size for the cedar chest. All he had to do was measure the bed. It would be as wide as the bed and not so tall that it would cover the beautiful scrollwork of the iron. It was such a beautiful bed!

It must be as deep, front to back, as a folded quilt. It was his own idea to put two small drawers at each end for the special little things a woman needs a place for.

The cedar boards planed up beautifully. The ancient trees had grown on a windswept hillside, and in their formative period, they had twisted as certain limbs grew faster than others, forcing patterns into the grain of the wood.

Numerous layers of shellac gave the chest the glossy appearance of being encased in glass and also prevented the cedar smell from coming out into the room. The untreated interior retained the smell, for protection from moths and silverfish. Counting the trip to Jacksonville, the chest cost Johnny more than three days, but if the weather did not stay too damp, the finish would be hard and dry by her birthday, the second of April. Anticipating her pleasure when she saw it, Johnny decided the three days and the milling fee were time and money well spent.

Louise came to have her dress fitted. The wide collar draped on her shoulders and the tucks fell to her hips in perfect rows. The wide skirt flared gracefully to her ankles, whispering against itself as she walked, and the color was stunning with her black hair.

While she was there, Louise pin-fitted Amy's dress. She stood tall and slim as a wax candle. The heavy satin molded against her back and shoulders with soft gathers at the neckline. Wide lace stood up, ruffled at the back of the neck and over her shoulders, framing her face like a portrait. The lace extended down the front of the dress where Gran's topaz pin clasped it firmly.

The fit of the skirt was straight and flat over her stomach and hips, ending in deep, flouncing gathers at the back. Scallops of filmy tulle drooped in folds across the stomach and ended in a massive bow. The wide ends of the bow were trimmed with lace and embroidered with sprigs of flowers, white on white, in the latest style. The delicate weight of the lace and embroidery caused the gauzy tulle to lay in feather-light folds.

The price of the dress came to $13.80 and Louise's dress was less than $8.00. They were both now finished, except for the final pressing, and it was only three days before the test in Jacksonville.

"I can't be seein' you, Johnny, so don't be thinkin' on tryin' to change my mind. I only got me two nights to study."

The River Bend Coal Company shut down the first of April. "Job's yours next year if you want it," they told him. Now he was free to haul rocks from the roadside and stumps from neighbor's fields to pitch into the soft mud. Load after back-breaking load sunk below the water, but he kept hauling.

Early on the morning of April 12, test day, Johnny came for Amy. During the three-hour trip to Jacksonville, Amy did not lift her eyes from the books. Spelling, then English, then spelling.

"Gonna have me some trouble," she prophesied. "Words don't spell like they sound and sentences don't go together like we say 'em. Come time I say sentences like they say to, folks'd think I was mad at 'em," she complained.

"Lookie at this'n. It says, 'You have a hole in your skirt.' First off, the book makes it sound like she tore that hole on purpose, to make a body point it out. If it was me, I'd say, 'Some old vine pulled a snag in your skirt when you went by'. That'd show I was sorry it happened, 'cause I had it happen to me, one time."

At Jacksonville, in the test room of the courthouse, she was led away with several others into a big room and the door was closed. With Amy locked behind the door, Johnny was restless. It would seem unfeeling of him to sit comfortably under the shade tree in the courtyard or to go the buggy and take a nap while she labored at something so important to her.

An hour passed and then another while Johnny walked up one street and down the other, checking the classroom at each trip. Finally, she emerged through the door, her face was pale but her cheeks were flushed red. Her hair was damp from perspiration and there was an ink smear on her cheek.

"Amy, you look awful! You gettin' sick or somethin'?"

Dismally, she nodded.

Johnny continued, "I been waitin' and watchin', thinkin' you'd be wantin' to get ice cream while we wait."

Her eyes flew open and her hand clamped over her mouth. "Don't say nothin' about eatin'. I feel strange in my stomach and I was scared I'd be messin' up their shiny floor in there. I think I'm a'fixin' to upchuck."

Johnny stared at this unknown person standing before him. "But, Amy...?"

"I got'a wait two hours or I got'a make the trip back tomorrow to see what I did. We gonna be mornin' gettin' home and I told Mr. Jenkins I'd be only needin' one day." The green eyes stared vacantly out of the pale face.

Johnny had been hungry for hours, but he was hungry no longer. Concern for her occupied all his senses. "What're you wantin' to do for two hours?"

"We got'a get you a suit to get married in so I reckon it ought'a be done right now."

"Me? A suit?"

"Yep, or it'll look a mite funny, me up there in all that white satin and you in your overhalls."

Johnny sighed with relief. This was the old Amy he knew and loved.

The sight of Johnny standing before her in the new suit completely took her mind off the test results. This suit would be perfect for the wedding at Five-Mile-Hill Community church, and later, would allow him to stand with pride in the River Bend Congregational Church where they would be attending after they were married.

Back on the street with the new suit in a big box, together with a new white shirt and a shiny necktie, Amy's heart was light and she breathed deeply. The aroma of the popcorn vender lured them.

Two bags, eaten while sitting on the benches in the courtyard took the edge off their hunger. A triple dip ice cream cone, topped it off.

"Look at that, five flavors, and the cone only holds three dips."

"Speck they want you to buy two cones. Like last time."

Feeling better, now, they giggled like school children on a holiday. Then the clock in the courthouse belfry sounded. Amy was stricken. She gasped and looked at the courthouse in a panic.

"Johnny, I'm gonna be sick. I know it."

"No, you ain't. You been eatin' all that popcorn and ice cream, and you ain't gonna undo all that, so just keep your mind off it. We got'a go get them test grades, right now."

An old gentleman with a flowing beard was sitting before the desk, writing names on large, white certificates. Names were called and the owner of the name went forward and listened to low, mumbled words and waited until the certificate was completed. Then each left, smiling, through the side door.

Amy sat stone still, her face ashen. Johnny sat with her, concerned, in spite of his brave words. This was a strange person sitting beside him. The test must have meant a sight more to her than he could have imagined.

"Amy Catherine Darnell."

"Yes, sir," and Amy stumbled forward.

"Miss Darnell, we have reviewed your grades and wondered if perhaps you have chosen the wrong profession. You have a perfect score in your math, and would, no doubt, make a good bookkeeper if you had a relative in some kind of business. However, you also did well in history and literature. Your English was acceptable, though much below your other scores. Your spelling is a concern. You passed the minimum standard, though with very little margin. It is our recommendation to you that, if you plan to use this certificate to teach, you should acquire a good dictionary and have it with you at all times."

Amy's heart was slamming against her throat, so it was only natural that she should have no voice. She nodded, yes, she would get a dictionary. Her breath stopped as she saw her name, Miss Amy Catherine Darnell, being written in beautiful script on the large, white sheet. She was now qualified to teach children from grades one through six. She had done it. Her breath returned just in time to keep her from falling to the floor in a heap. She had held to the edge of the table for support, and now, with great effort, she released the table, and took her certificate. She looked back at Johnny and he was grinning from ear to ear. He stood and waited for her and they left the room.

"Johnny, lookie here! I have it!"

"I know, Amy. I was in there. You did good."

"Not on spelling. I didn't do good, at all."

"Looks good to me. You passed and that's more'n I'd'a done."

"I got'a get a dictionary."

"Amy, it's dark outside and the stores ain't open. Ain't there a dictionary in that catalog?"

"Reckon so. Johnny, how about the cows? Likely bawlin' their heads off, wantin' to be milked."

"Likely, but there was pain to be felt by either on you or them, and 'twixt the two, I figured you was a'hurtin' the most. Trip home'll be fast, Brushy wantin' his grain."

They settled into the buggy, and Brushy jogged along while they ate the leftovers from the picnic basket, then Amy leaned back and closed her eyes, while Johnny watched. Her hand, clasping the certificate, relaxed and the precious white paper slid to the buggy floor.

"Amy?"

There was no answer. Johnny took both reins and wound them onto the holder, allowing Brushy to decide on his own gait. His arm circled the sleeping girl and drew her down with her head in his lap. Poor, exhausted Amy. Another week, honey, and you'll be mine. With that promise to himself, Johnny leaned back and closed his eyes.

Brushy turned suddenly at the gate of the cabin, and the rough driveway woke them.

"My certificate! Johnny, we lost it!"

"No, we got it. It's on the floorboard."

"Oh. I got it, now. Oh, Johnny, listen at them poor cows out there, bawlin'. I can take the buggy and let you get to 'em. I thought I'd be jumpin' up and down excited when I got my certificate but all I am is bone-tired. You know what I mean?"

"No, Amy, I don't know what you mean, but then I didn't take that test." Johnny stepped from the buggy and slapped Brushy's firm rear. The pony headed toward the livery, his second home.

24

IT WAS VERY late on Thursday evening, three days before her wedding, and the candle still burned in Amy's room.

"Gran, I can't do it. Now the time's come, and I can't look it in the eye. I need you here to talk sense into me. I keep thinkin' on things I need to ask, but you left me."

The loneliness became unbearable and she turned her face to the pillow and began to sob. "I can't, Gran, I can't," she told the pillow. She drew herself into a dejected ball of misery and pulled the bed sheet over her head. She'd tell Johnny tomorrow that she just couldn't do it. There was too much she didn't know. Maybe another year and she'd be ready. "Oh, Gran, Gran," she wailed, smothering her words into the feathers.

A light tap sounded at the door and she sat up, quickly, gouging fists into wet eyes. "Come in."

Mrs. Thomason nudged the door open with her toe because her hands were full. She carried two cups with whiffs of steam rising.

"Amy, honey, I heard you in here not sleepin', bein' natural to do at this time in your life. Got us some hot chocolate, like what I always want when I'm anxious."

The girl took the hot drink, gratefully, warming her icy fingers on the cup.

"Shame, you not havin' your mama or your Gran here when you get to feelin' down, likely more'n you ever will again in your whole life."

She sipped the sweet chocolate, sitting cross-legged on her bed.

Mrs. Thomason smiled, "Puts me in the mind of the time when I was to marry. Didn't hardly even know 'im, like you do your Johnny. Said to my ma, 'I hate 'im, and I ain't gonna ever marry 'im. If you make me to it, I'll be thinkin' on a way to kill 'im'."

Amy smiled at the thought of kind Mrs. Thomason killing her thoughtful husband.

"Cryin' all night gave me red eyes, and still I had to be standin' there in front of the preacher. Must'a been a sight, enough to cause him to laugh."

Now Amy chuckled. "Reckon I ain't quite that bad. I was just wantin' to put it off a year."

Mrs. Thomason examined the hem of Amy's wedding dress as it hung by the door.

"A good hand for sewin', you got, honey. Your Gran done herself some good teachin' on that hand work. I like them new machine stitches, too. They seem solid, like. Reckon I'll have to think on gettin' me one of them machines and have you teach me to work it."

Amy brightened at the thought. "Be no problem to me, Miz. Thomason. You'd be sewin' in no time, flat."

The older woman nodded. "Gonna do that in a month or so. Child, that chocolate done made me too sleepy to hold open my eyes. Reckon I better get on to bed."

"Goodnight, Miz. Thomason." Amy, now warm and relaxed, eased down to her pillow and drifted into sleep.

Miz. Thompson returned to her bed.

"Givin' comfort to the bride?" he asked her.

"Yep. Been in there spinnin' yarns about how scared I was 'afore you and I got married." Then she chuckled.

He nudged her playfully with his elbow. "You mean you weren't sayin' to her how I sneaked you out'a your bedroom window and run off with you in the middle'a the night, and you lovin' every minute of it? And us wakin' up the preacher man at six o'clock in the morning, anxious to be married before God and man? You wasn't sayin' that to her?"

"No. I thought she might not need to know the whole truth, leastways not right now."

"You told that girl somethin' that wasn't true?" he teased.

"It weren't so bad as all that. It's the way I'd'a been feelin', for sure, if I had'a married the fellow my folks picked out."

"Relieved to know I didn't make no mistake, pickin' you." Mr. Thomason reached out from under the sheet and lovingly stroked his wife's snowwhite hair and her multiple chins.

25

IT WAS LATE on Friday that Johnny delivered Amy to her mother. There were many things to get done on the Saturday before the wedding, and Louise brought her baby and spent the day, helping with the many details.

The warm, April sun shining on her face woke the bride on her wedding day. She lay in bed and listened to the sounds. Doors opened and shut, the sound of the cream separator droned on. Birds sang. This was her last day to be Amy Darnell.

After breakfast, she piled her hair high and put her dress and veil in the buggy. The wedding would be directly after the church service. The small, wooden building of Five-Mile Community Church was crowded full. Weddings always brought out a lot of people.

Then, finally, Amy and Louise stood together at the back door of the church, waiting for the pump organ to begin the wedding song. A huge, yellow butterfly circled Louise's head, then lit on the yellow daisies she carried.

"Look! How did that butterfly get in?"

The insect flexed its wings but did not fly away. Then another one came in, settling on the shiny curls of Louise's hair, and it was now time to walk toward the preacher.

Halfway down the aisle, the butterfly took to its wings. It hovered above the aisle until Amy approached, then settled on the topaz pin

The bride looked down at the butterfly as she walked to the alter where Johnny, resplendent in his new suit, waited for her. The butterfly flitted from the pin to the daisies she carried. It startled up and circled her head, lighting again on the flowers.

Amy heard the words of the ceremony only as a murmur, and not related to her. She said "yes" she would take Johnny as her husband. How strange it would be if she said she wouldn't, after all the trouble she'd gone to? Then she heard the preacher say, "I now pronounce you man and wife." She gazed down at the shiny gold ring Johnny was slipping on her finger, the ring to be remembered in the shiny yellow thread in the center block of Gran's quilt. *I got that ring, now, Gran.*

Louise took the armful of yellow daisies from her, and the butterfly rode along. She turned toward smiling faces. Rice began falling around her and hugs and laughter were everywhere.

The butterflies left the flowers and clung to the safety of Louise's mound of black curls, covering the top of her head. They appeared to be exquisite hair ornaments, exactly matching the color of her dress.

Finally, Amy and Johnny were in the buggy. Someone had tied old shoes and other junk behind it. They always did that. Whoever was it that saved up old shoes for the occasion? No one she knew, but they were always there.

Everyone was invited to the Darnell's for cake, and somewhere along the way, the butterflies took leave of the bride.

Later, Amy and Johnny left the Darnell's to go home to their cabin. Five buggies followed them down the hill. The five brothers. Amy expected them.

"Johnny?"

"Yeah?"

"You take note of them butterflies at the weddin'?"

"Been hard not to."

"Odd, for 'em to come into the church buildin' that'a'way, with that crowd of people and all."

"Sure was."

"You'd'a thought they'd been scared and flown away."

"Sure would'a."

"Johnny, I sure wisht Gran could'a been there."

"Me, too."

"You 'member Gran sayin' that sometimes I reminded her of the yellow butterflies when I was little? Flittin' here and there?"

"Sure do."

There was along pause, the only sound being the song of the birds in the trees and the sound of the buggy and Brushy's feet. The five buggies behind them stretched out over a quarter of a mile back.

"Johnny, Gran sure did want to see us get married. I keep thinkin' of them butterflies, actin' strange."

"You thinkin' Gran sent them butterflies to see how things went, then to come and tell her?"

"Sounds like what Gran'd do, if she could. Wonder why there was two of 'em, and why they liked Louise's hair."

"Reckon maybe she thought two butterflies'd be able to see twice as much, and Louise's hair was a good place to watch from?"

"Be as good'a guess as any."

The buggy had now reached the bottom of the hill and turned west on the river road. Johnny was restless. The five wagons were still there. Their presence boded no good.

"I sure dread whatever them fellows got planned up for me," Johnny complained. "A shivaree ain't no fun, less'n you're the one to get to play the tricks. Bein' the fellow that just got married, that turns the tale around."

"They ain't gonna do nothin'. Dave promised me."

"I don't care what Dave said, they'll be doin' somethin'."

"No, they ain't. He promised."

"After what I did to Dave? No way he'd let me get away 'thout doin' somethin'."

"But he promised."

"What exact words did he say?"

"He said, 'Don't worry, sis. We promise we ain't gonna do nothin' to you'."

"See there? I knew it! 'Course, they ain't gonna do nothin' to you. It's me they're gonna do somethin' to."

His bride considered the matter and nodded. "Reckon you should'a thought'a this a'happenin', 'afore you threw them walnuts on their tin roof all night long. Flingin' 'em in the pond could'a been a better thing for you to'a done."

Brushy turned in at the new driveway and the five other buggies followed, totally filling the small yard. Five brothers and five wives came in at Amy's cool invitation. The cabin was admired and the gifts commented on. Store bought creme mints were eaten. Conversation lagged, but still they stayed on. It was getting late.

Finally she changed out of her wedding dress. The lace itched her neck.

The fellows wanted to see Johnny's pole barn, so she made fresh coffee and opened a tin of store bought cookies. The wives looked at the catalog, marveling at the things one could buy, that no one had any use for.

Then the three oldest brothers collected their wives and left. Louise and Addie Mae admired Amy's cedar quilt chest and the fancy iron bed. It began to get dark, so she lit two candles.

Finally, Willie and Dave came for their wives. "Sis, Johnny's gonna be tied up for a while, thought bein' as he was out there, he might as well finish up what needed to be done."

Amy nodded and waved them away, and then sat down to wait for Johnny. She made fresh coffee and a sandwich. It had been so long since lunch, Johnny was sure to be hungry. The candle burned low, as she looked at the catalog. She swept up the crumbs from the store bought cookies. She lit another candle. What was keeping Johnny so long? How much time did it take to feed the horses and turn them out?

Then she heard Brushy snort and rattle his harness, impatiently. Something was wrong. Johnny wouldn't leave Brushy in the harness this long. She stepped outside but could see nothing in the pitch blackness. Brushy snorted again and stomped his feet.

Amy lit the lantern and walked around the house to the horse barn.

"Johnny?" No answer.

She stepped inside the dark barn. There were the Clydesdales, eating corn from their feedbox.

"Johnny?" Still no answer. "Where are you, Johnny?"

A strange noise came from the feed room. Amy went in, tiptoeing cautiously. It was empty.

"Johnny?"

There was the noise, again. She looked around. There, on a peg on the wall, hung Johnny's wedding coat. On another peg was his trousers.

"Johnny, where are you?"

The noise came from the corncrib. Cautiously, Amy opened the lid. There was Johnny's head, right there on top of the shelled corn. She screamed in horror, but there was the noise again, and the head wagged from side to side.

She held the light so she could see better, then she took the gag from his mouth. Words burst forth.

"I'll get 'im! I know I'll get 'im!" yelled Johnny, after the gag was removed. "Help me get out. Them brothers'a yours tied me up and buried me in here. It was Dave's idea and I'm a'gonna get 'im."

Amy dipped corn into a barrel until she could see to untie Johnny's hands and feet. Then she said, solemnly, "Don't worry, Johnny, I'll get 'im."

"No, I want'a get 'im," insisted the injured groom.

But the bride was presistant. "He's mine, I tell you. He done messed up my weddin'." Her lips were firm and her chin dimple could have been carved in stone.

By now, Johnny was out of the corncrib and was putting on his suit. "No, he didn't mess up the weddin'. I want you to go in the house and put on your weddin' dress, then get back in the buggy. I'll put away Brushy and come and get you, then we gonna do this right."

"Sit in the buggy...?"

"Yep, this is my only weddin' and I'm gonna do it right."

Amy went. She was sitting in the buggy in her white satin dress when Johnny, dressed again in his suit, came to unhitch Brushy and take him to the barn. He came back and, leaning into the buggy, gathered his bride in his arms.

"Gonna do it right," he muttered again, as Amy, in Johnny's arms, turned the doorknob on the fancy new store-bought door. Johnny kicked back the door with his heel and carried his bride across the threshold. "Then I'm gonna get Dave."

Amy, still in Johnny's arms, assured him. "I'll get Dave. I got a better way. Every year, he forgets Louise's birthday, and I have to remind him. This year I won't. Whatever you was plannin' to do to him, it ain't nothin' compared to what Louise'll do, time he forgets her birthday!"

The candle was now burning low, about to gutter itself out. Johnny carried her to the table and she leaned down and snuffed out the flickering flame.

"You're right," Johnny agreed, finally. Silence.

"He's your brother, you get to get 'im," he told the dark room.

The sliver of a lover's moon could be seen through the shiny plate glass window and Johnny was still holding Amy.

And the river rolled on.